PROGRESSIVE INDEPENDENCE: ROCK

A Comprehensive Guide To Basic Rock And Funk Drumming

By Ron Spagnardi

Design And Layout By Joe King
Cover Photo Courtesy of Tama Drums
© Copyright 2000 Modern Drummer Publications, Inc.
International Copyright Secured
Printed In The USA

Second Printing 2010

Published By:
Modern Drummer Publications, Inc.
12 Old Bridge Road
Cedar Grove, NJ 07009 USA

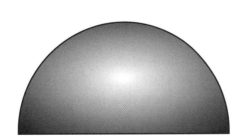

CONTENTS

CD track listing can be found on page 164.

INTRODUCTION

*P*rogressive Independence: Rock is designed to help you gain an extremely high level of coordinated independence for rock drumming performance, thereby freeing all four limbs from dependence on one another. Once the material in this book has been mastered, you'll be capable of playing almost *any* rhythmic figure on snare and bass drum, in combination with six varied hi-hat/cymbal patterns, while the hi-hat foot plays quarter notes, 8th notes, or upbeat 8ths.

Progressive Independence: Rock is structured in a very straightforward manner. Each of the book's six sections offers a selection of snare drum and bass drum rhythms using six different hi-hat/cymbal patterns. Starting with 8th notes and then quarter-note hi-hat/cymbal patterns, the book moves on to 8th-note upbeats, 16th notes, and two common 16th-note figures. Part 1 of each section deals strictly with snare drum independence. Part 2 focuses on the bass drum only. In Part 3, snare and bass drum combination patterns are presented with left-foot quarter notes. Part 4 adds left-foot hi-hat 8th notes to the previous exercises, and Part 5 presents upbeat hi-hat 8th notes. In Part 6, two-bar combinations are demonstrated using the three previously learned hi-hat patterns.

How To Practice This Book

1) Pay *close* attention to the four separate parts of each exercise. Each should be played *precisely* as written.

2) Beginners may want to omit the hi-hat foot part during the early stages of the book, and focus strictly on the two hands and bass drum coordination. Once facility with the three-way independence has been acquired, go back and add the hi-hat foot part.

3) Note that throughout the book, the right hand may be played on the ride cymbal *or* on closed hi-hat. Play the right hand on closed hi-hat when the hi-hat foot part is omitted. Play the right hand on the ride cymbal when the hi-hat foot part is played.

4) Be sure that *all* ghost notes (indicated in parentheses) are played much *softer* than the accented notes, and at roughly 2" off the drumhead.

5) *Repeat* all of the exercises ten to fifteen times. All parts should fall naturally among the limbs, and each exercise should be played in a relaxed, musical manner.

6) Practice each pattern *slowly* at first. Do not increase the tempo until each exercise can be played accurately and smoothly. Do not move on to the next pattern until the previous one has been mastered.

7) Practice this material with a metronome or drum machine to ensure a steady time flow and to gauge your progress as your facility increases.

8) Be *patient.* Achieving coordinated independence takes time, but is well worth the effort.

9) The following abbreviations are used throughout this book:

HH: Hi-Hat Hand; **CYMB:** Cymbal; **SD:** Snare Drum;
BD: Bass Drum; **HHF:** Hi-Hat Foot.

SECTION 1
Part 1: Snare Drum Independence With 8th Notes

In Part 1, straight 8th notes are played on the hi-hat or cymbal. The bass drum is played on 1 and 3 throughout, with the hi-hat on 1, 2, 3, and 4 of every measure. The snare drum part is varied in each of the following thirty patterns, starting out simply and gradually increasing in complexity.

Be sure to make a strong distinction between the ghost notes indicated in parentheses and the accents on 2 and 4. Take each pattern slowly at first and do not increase the tempo until you're certain you are playing the pattern correctly. Repeat each exercise ten to fifteen times before proceeding.

Progressive Independence: Rock

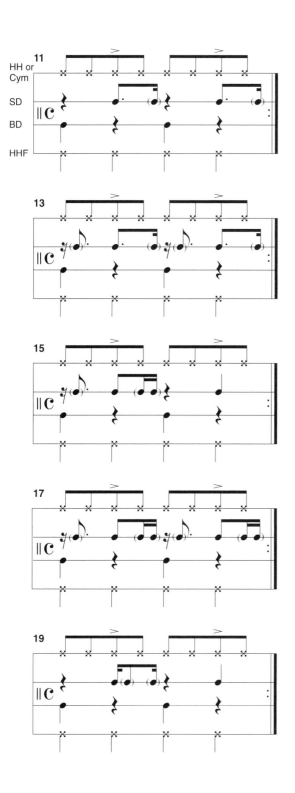
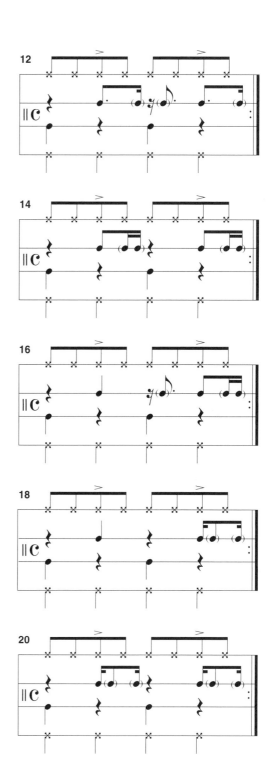

SECTION 1

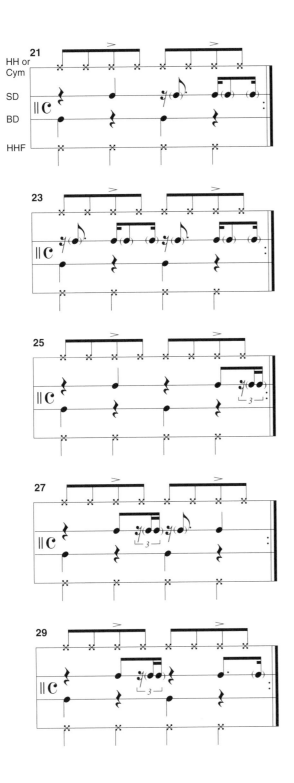
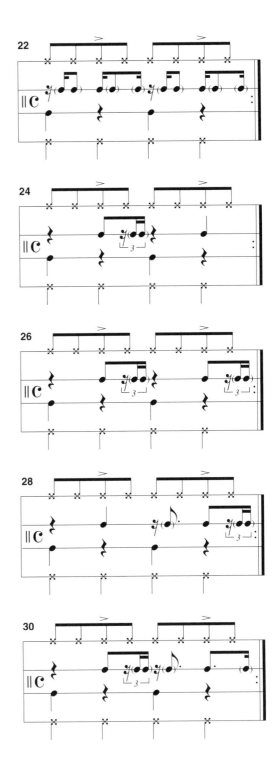

Progressive Independence: Rock

Part 2: Bass Drum Independence With 8th Notes

Part 2 introduces thirty varied bass drum patterns with 8th notes on the hi-hat or cymbal, 2 and 4 on the snare drum, and the hi-hat on every count. Similar to Part 1, the following bass drum patterns begin simply and increase in difficulty as you proceed. Again, avoid increasing the tempo until you can perform each exercise smoothly and accurately. Repeat each pattern ten to fifteen times before going on.

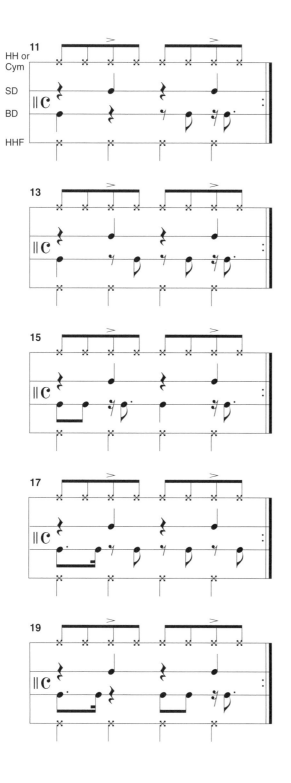

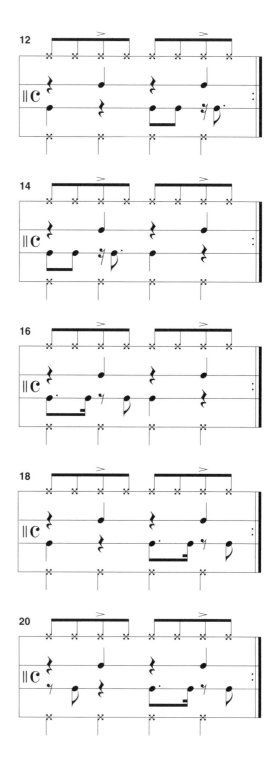

Progressive Independence: Rock

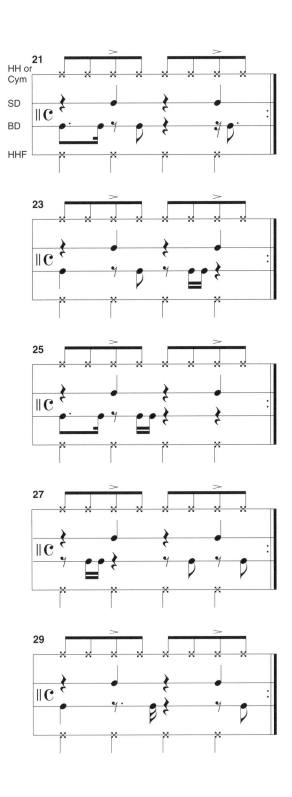
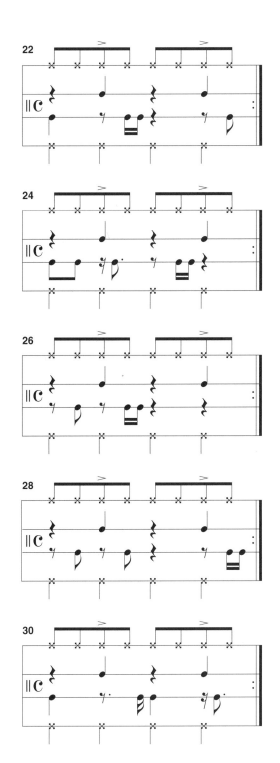

SECTION 1

Part 3: Snare Drum/Bass Drum Combination Patterns

Part 3 combines many of the snare drum variations in Part 1 with the bass drum patterns presented in Part 2. Take your time with the following combination exercises; they become increasingly more difficult as you proceed. Be sure to master each one before moving on to the next.

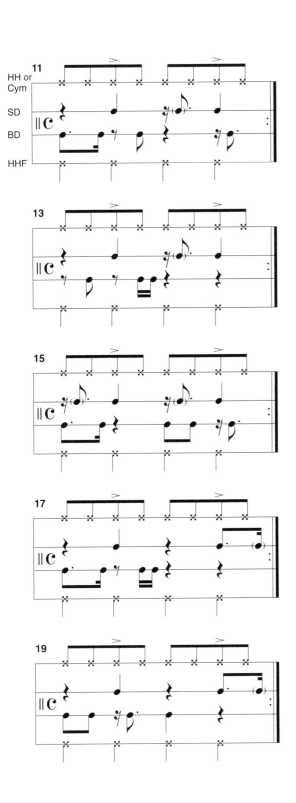
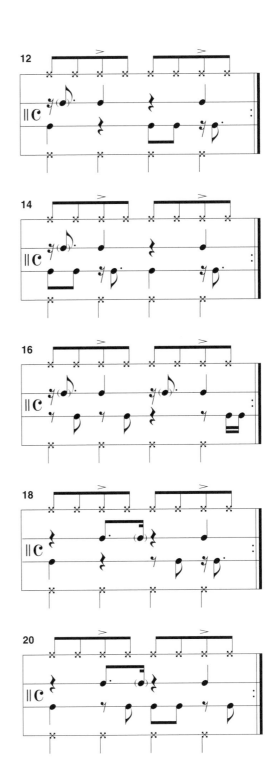

SECTION 1

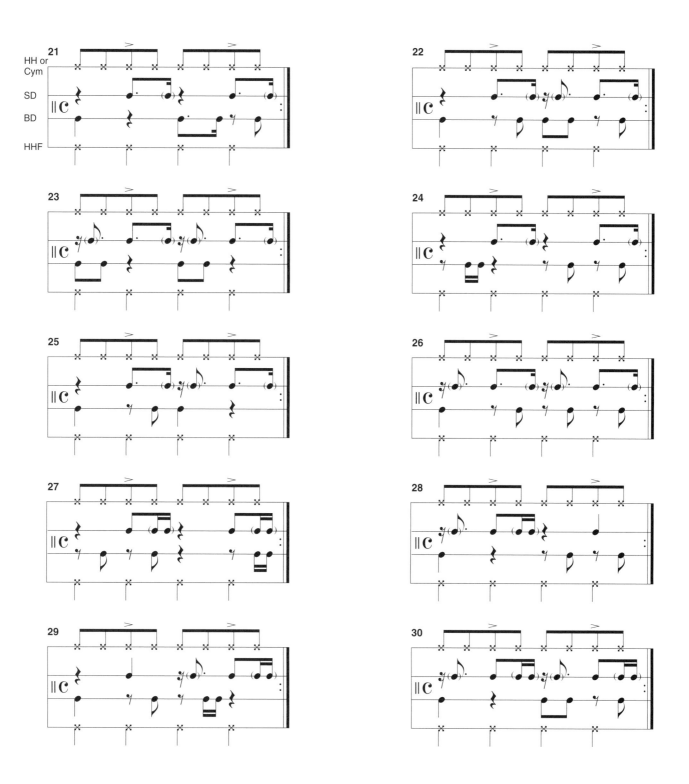

Progressive Independence: Rock

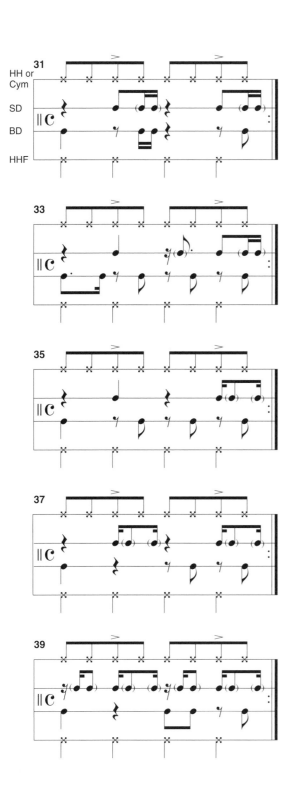

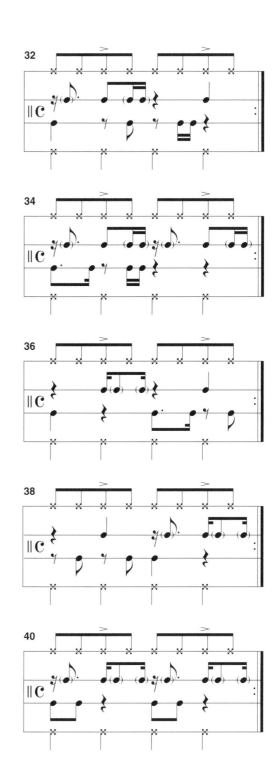

SECTION 1

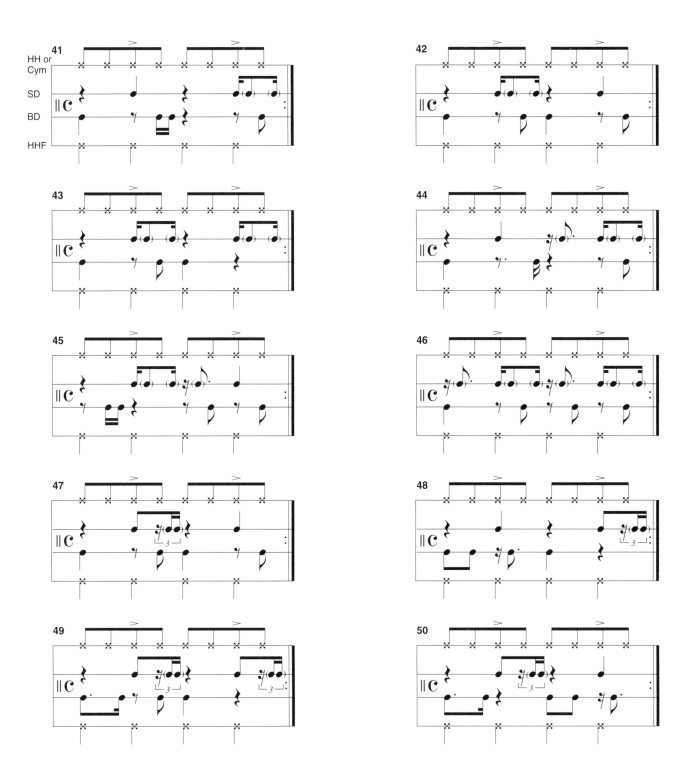

14

Progressive Independence: Rock

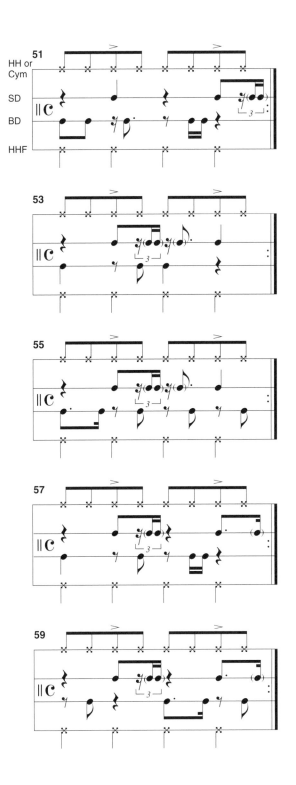
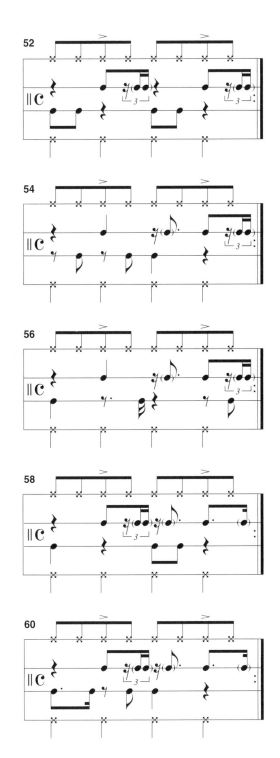

15

SECTION 1

Part 4: Snare Drum/Bass Drum Combination Patterns With Hi-Hat 8th Notes

In Part 4 the hi-hat foot now plays 8th notes throughout. Playing hi-hat 8th notes gives each exercise a different sound and feel, as well as presenting an advanced technical challenge. Take these exercises slowly and strive for accuracy. Use a metronome or a drum machine to ensure a smooth, even time flow.

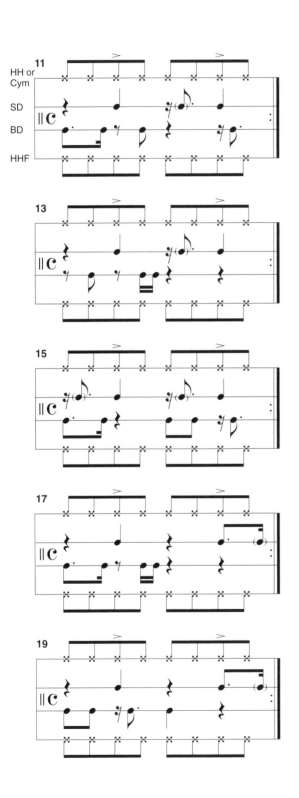
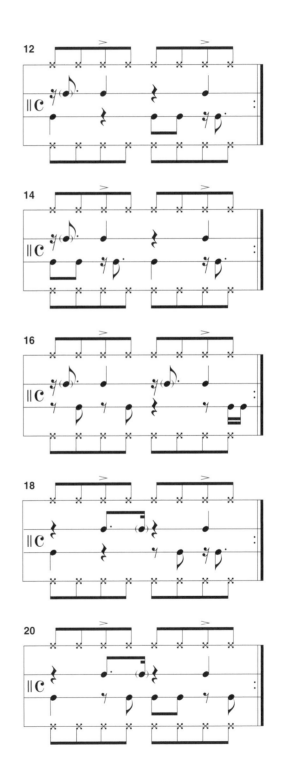

SECTION 1

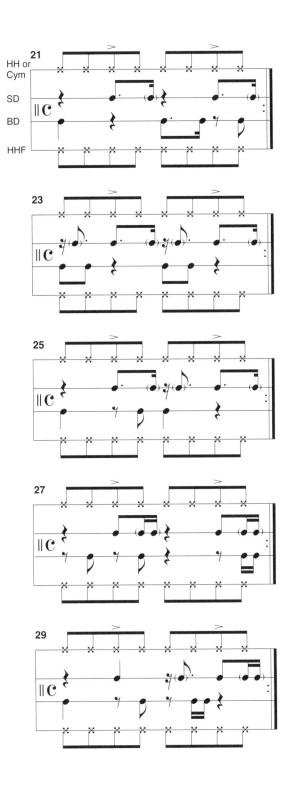
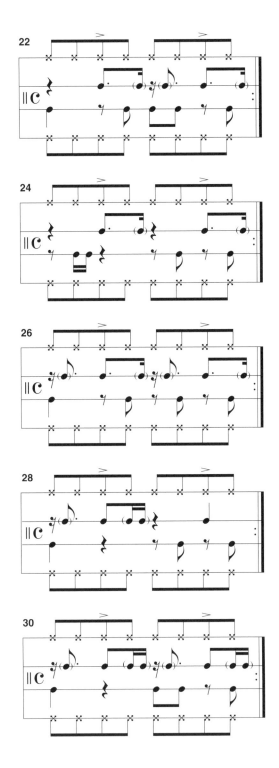

Progressive Independence: Rock

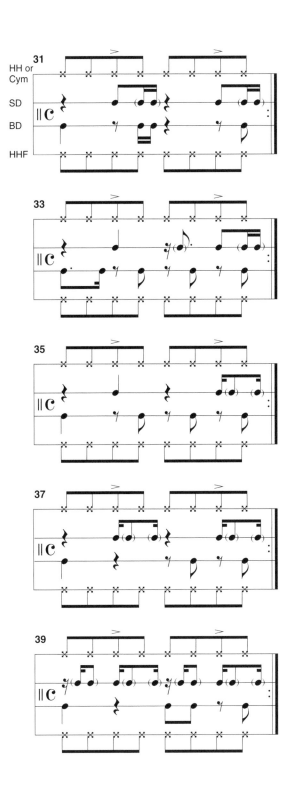
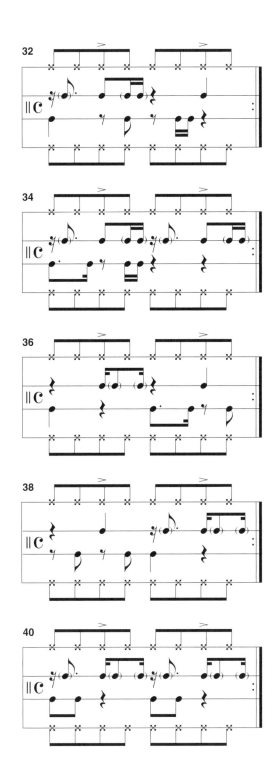

19

SECTION 1

Progressive Independence: Rock

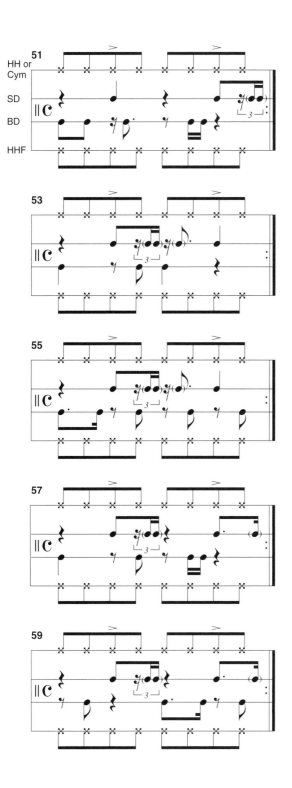
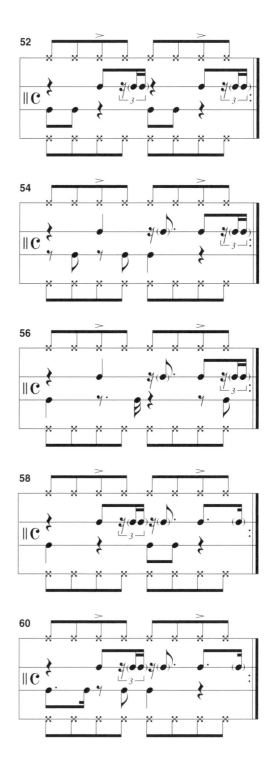

SECTION 1

Part 5: Snare Drum/Bass Drum Combination Patterns With Hi-Hat Upbeats

In this final part using 8th notes on the hi-hat or cymbal, the hi-hat foot now plays upbeat 8th notes. These patterns can be quite challenging, so take your time.

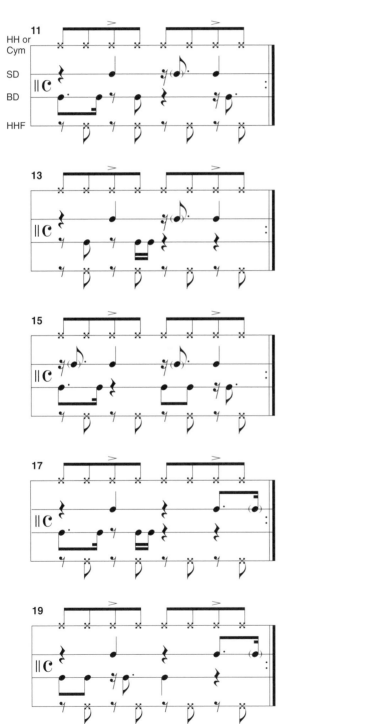
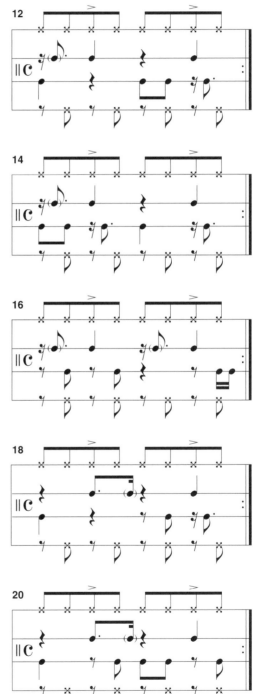

SECTION 1

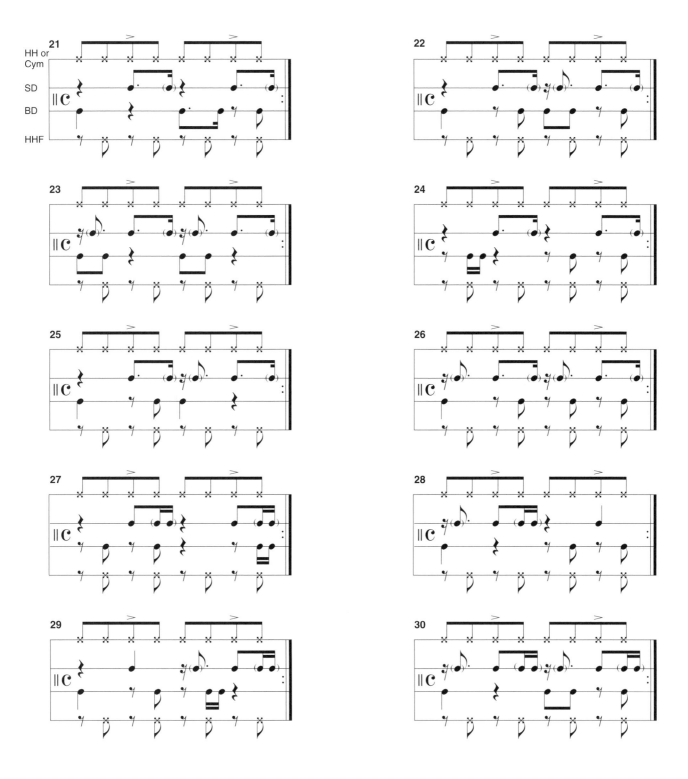

Progressive Independence: Rock

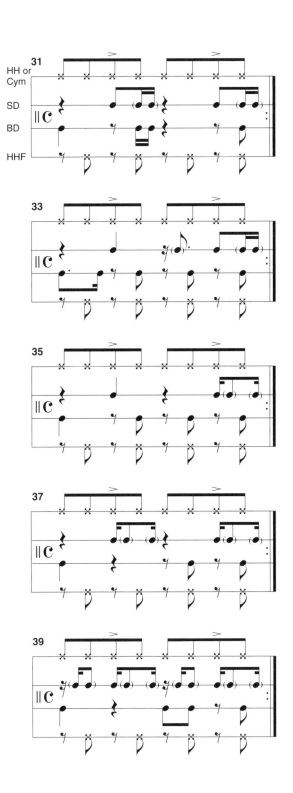
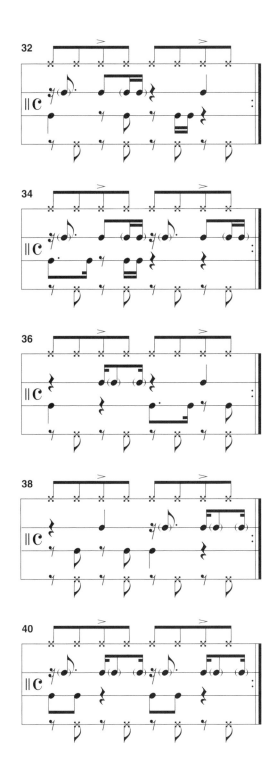

SECTION 1

Progressive Independence: Rock

SECTION 1

Part 6: Two-Bar Combinations

The following patterns are two-bar combinations of the previous material. Exercises 1 through 5 begin with hi-hat quarter notes. Practice these slowly at first, gradually increasing the tempo as your facility increases.

The five two-bar combination patterns below utilize hi-hat 8th notes.

Exercises 11 through 15 on this page have the hi-hat foot playing upbeat 8th notes.

SECTION 2
Part 1: Snare Drum Independence With Quarter Notes

Now we're going to use quarter notes on the hi-hat or cymbal with the same thirty snare drum variations presented previously. Note that the bass drum once again plays on the 1 and 3 of each measure, with the hi-hat on quarter notes. A strong distinction in volume between the accents and the ghost notes is absolutely essential. Repeat each pattern ten to fifteen times before moving on.

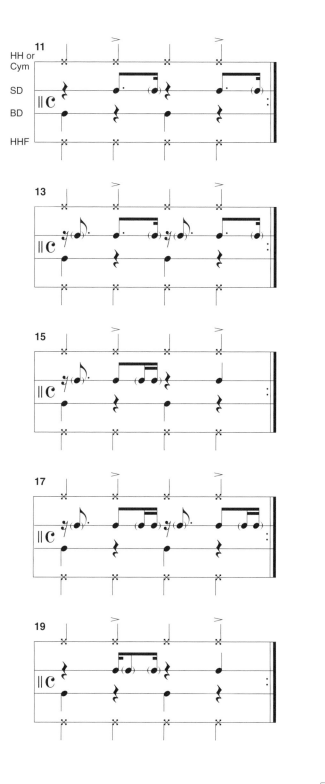
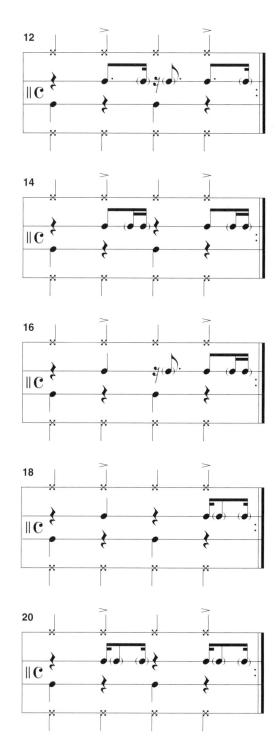

Progressive Independence: Rock

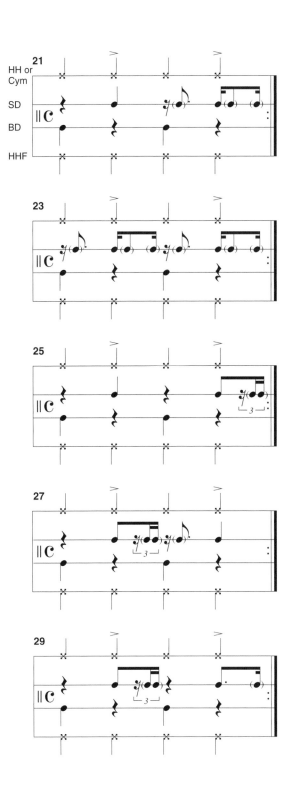
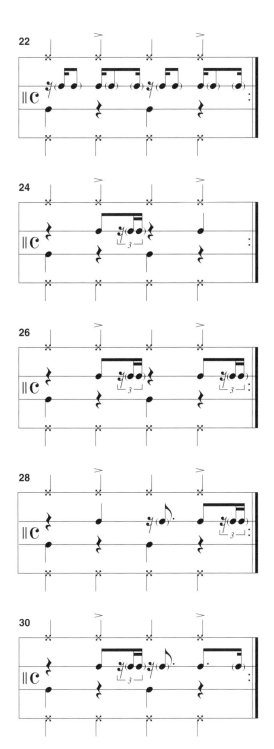

SECTION 2

Part 2: Bass Drum Independence With Quarter Notes

The same thirty bass drum variations used previously with 8th notes are again applied here. Be sure to maintain a strong accent on the 2 and 4 of each exercise. Feel free to omit the hi-hat foot part if you have difficulty with any of the patterns. Once you've gained facility with the three-way independence, go back and add the hi-hat part.

Progressive Independence: Rock

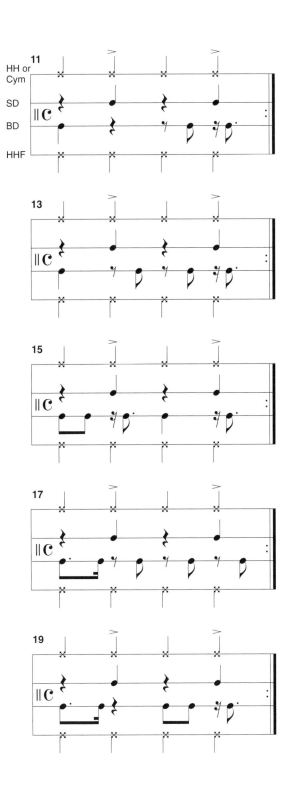
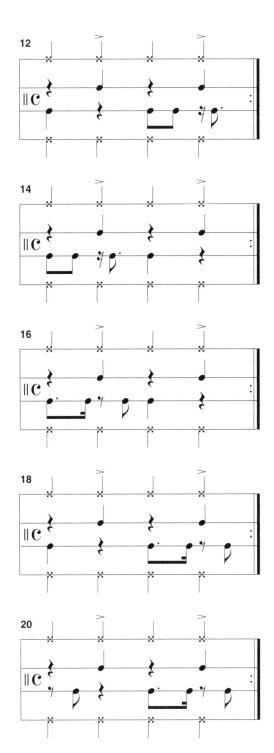

SECTION 2

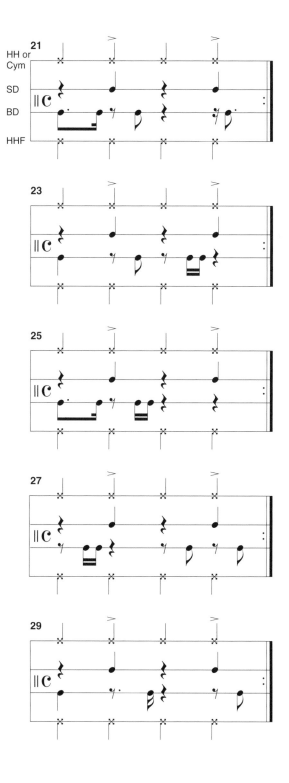
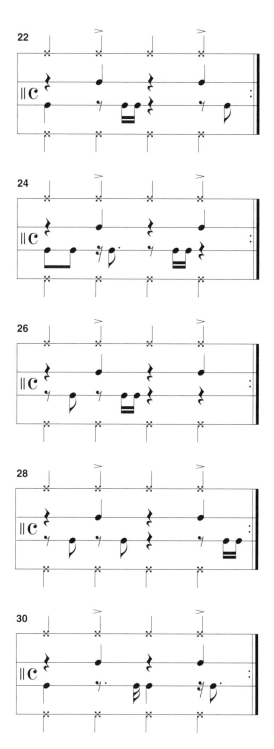

Progressive Independence: Rock

Part 3: Snare Drum/Bass Drum Combination Patterns

The following exercises combine the previous snare drum and bass drum patterns with quarter notes on the hi-hat or cymbal. Remember to play all ghost notes much softer than the accented notes.

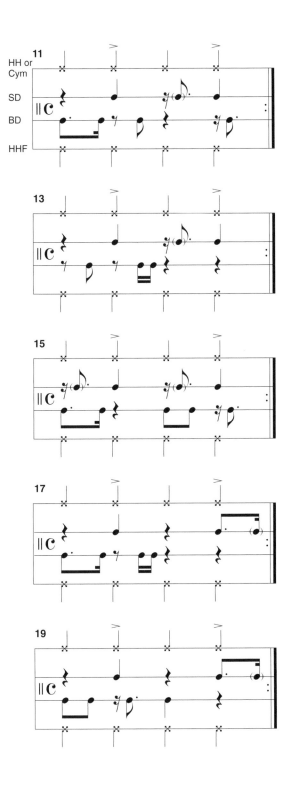
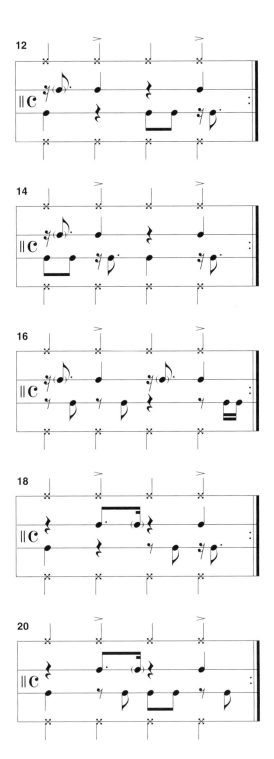

Progressive Independence: Rock

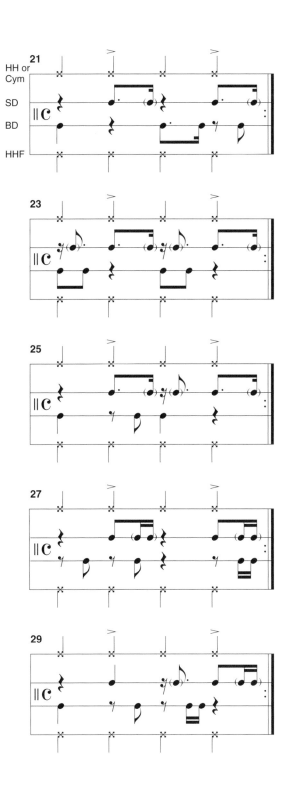
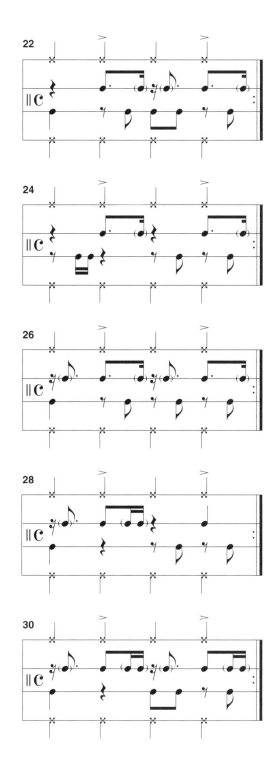

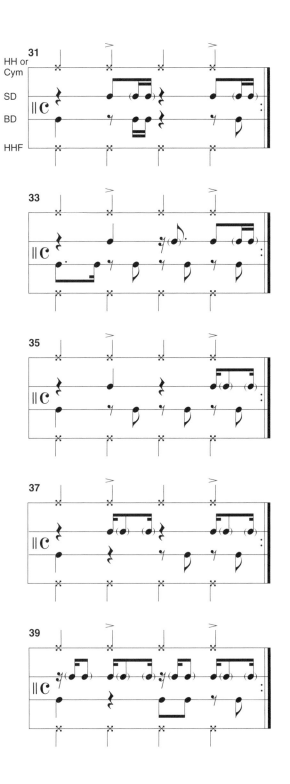
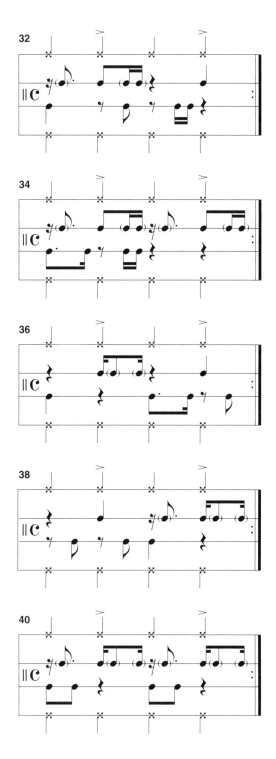

Progressive Independence: Rock

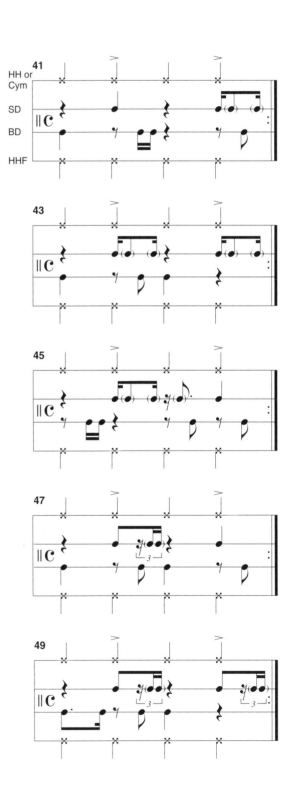
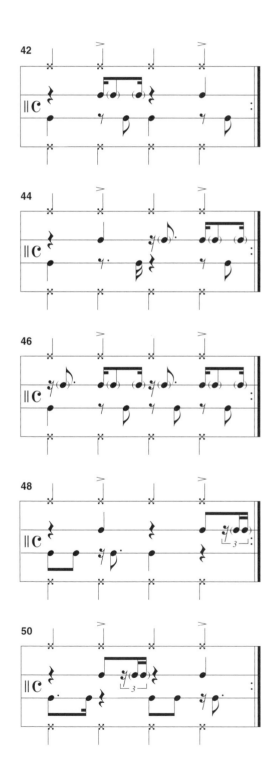

41

SECTION 2

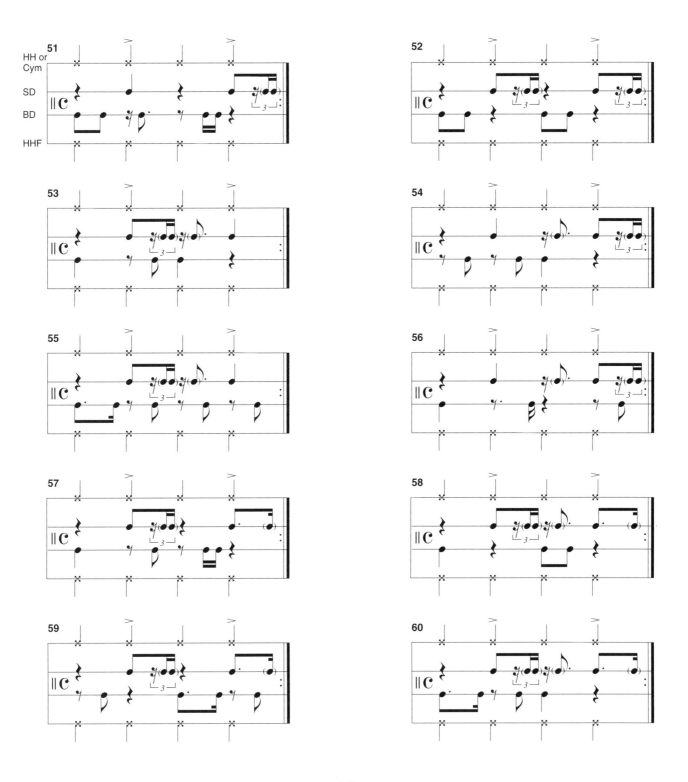

Progressive Independence: Rock

Part 4: Snare Drum/Bass Drum Combinations With Hi-Hat 8th Notes

Part 4 is a duplication of Part 3, but with the hi-hat now playing 8th notes throughout. The more complex hi-hat part will require increased concentration and technical fluency.

43

SECTION 2

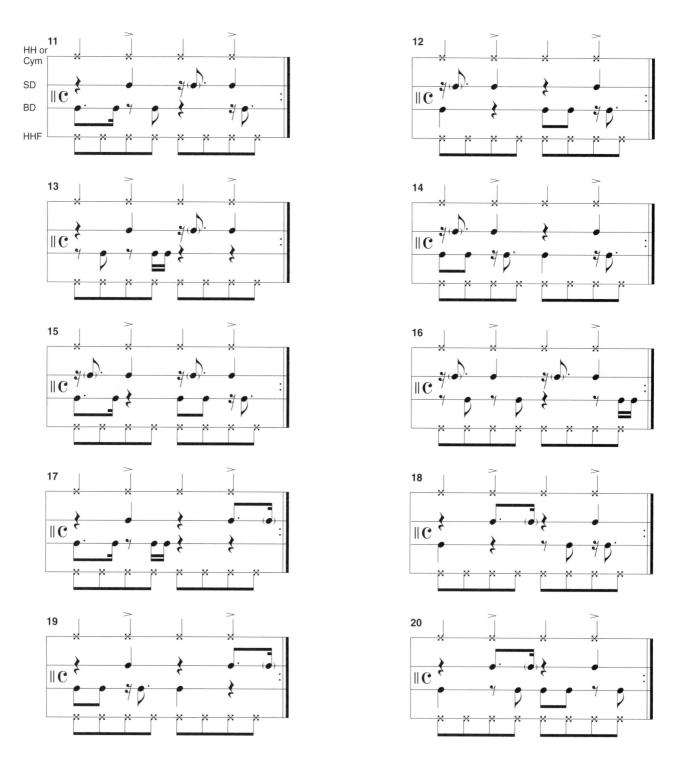

Progressive Independence: Rock

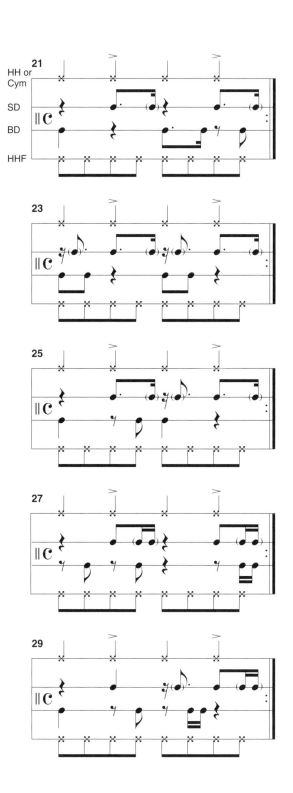
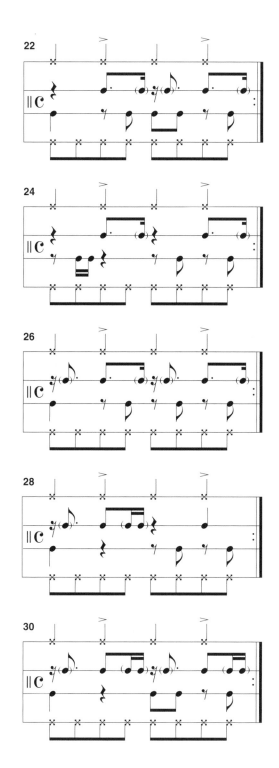

SECTION 2

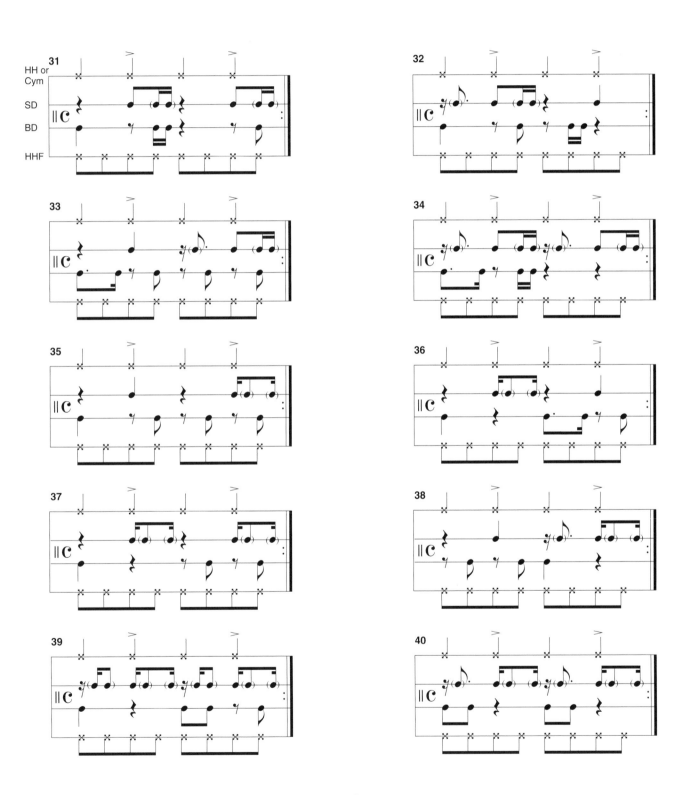

Progressive Independence: Rock

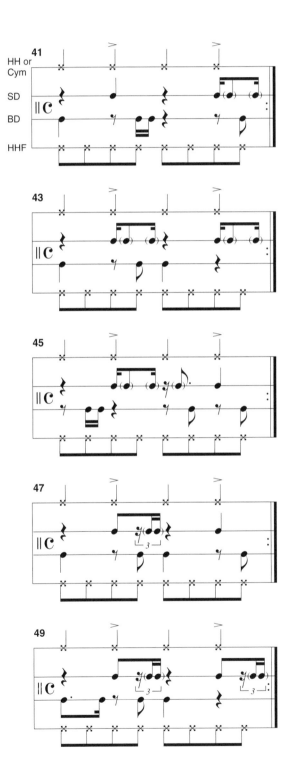
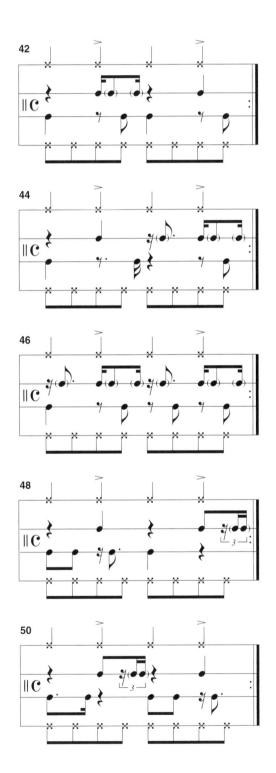

47

SECTION 2

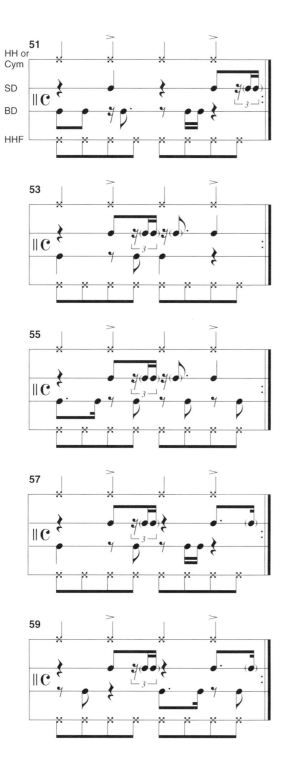
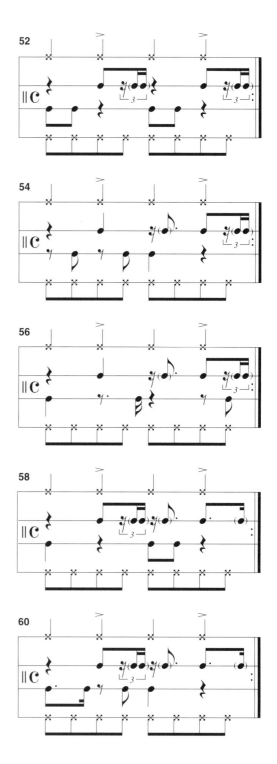

Progressive Independence: Rock

Part 5: Snare Drum/Bass Drum Combination Patterns With Hi-Hat Upbeats

Part 5 once again involves the use of upbeat 8th notes in the hi-hat foot part. These patterns can be challenging, so take your time. Use a metronome or drum machine to ensure a steady, even time flow. Repeat each pattern ten to fifteen times before moving on.

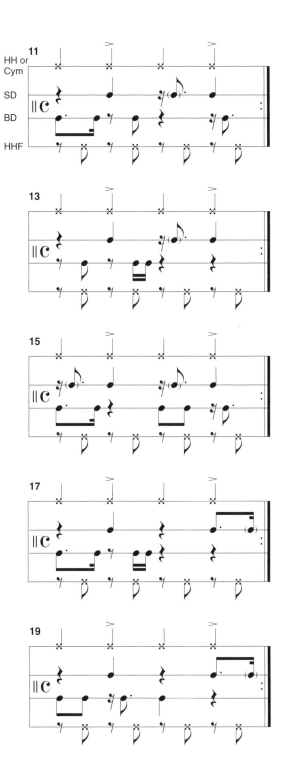

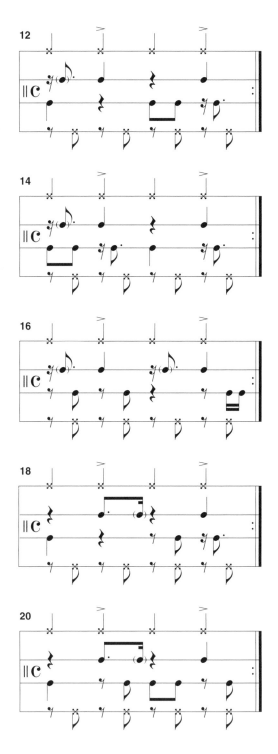

Progressive Independence: Rock

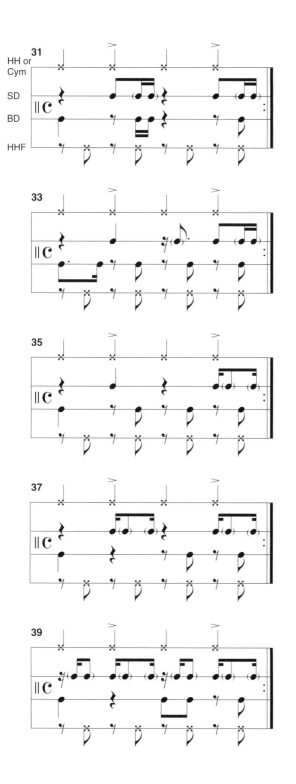
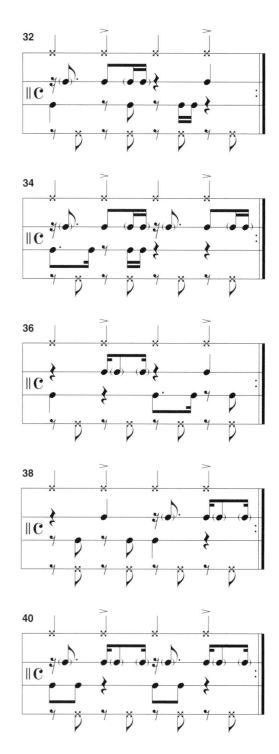

Progressive Independence: Rock

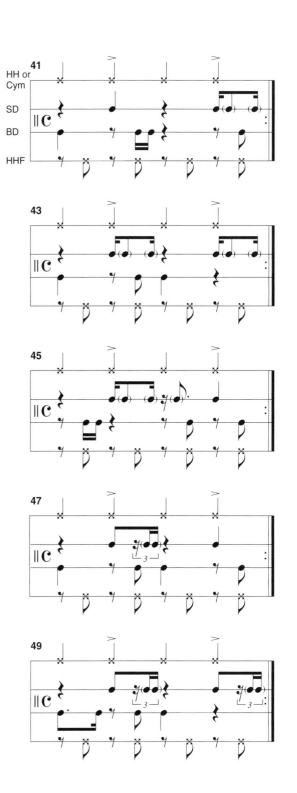
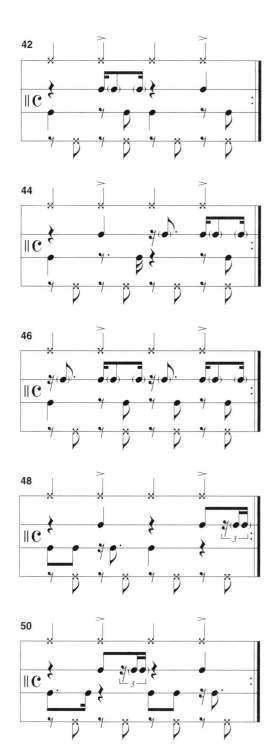

SECTION 2

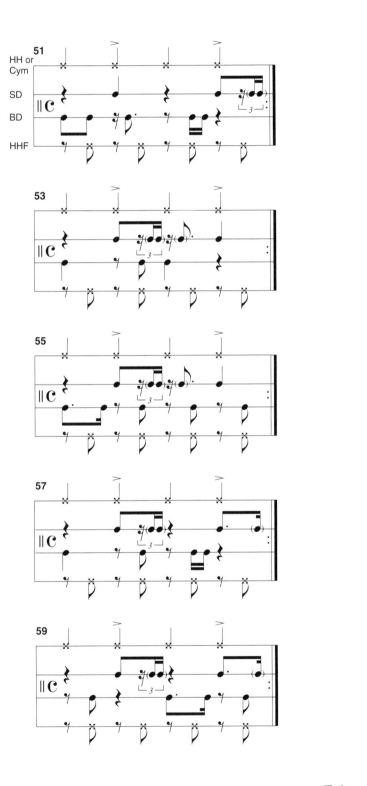
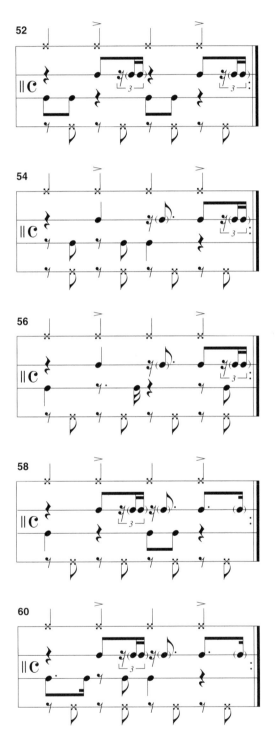

Progressive Independence: Rock

Part 6: Two-Bar Combinations

The following patterns are two-bar combinations of the previous material. Exercises 1 through 5 begin with hi-hat quarter notes. Practice these slowly at first, gradually increasing the tempo as your facility increases.

The five two-bar combination patterns below utilize hi-hat 8th notes.

Progressive Independence: Rock

Exercises 11 through 15 on this page have the hi-hat foot playing upbeat 8th notes.

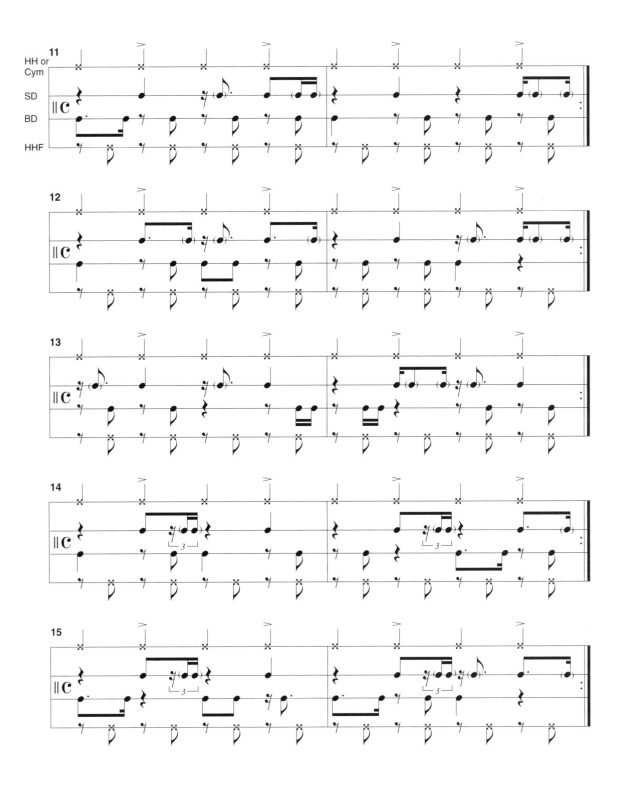

SECTION 2

SECTION 3

Part 1: Snare Drum Independence With 8th-Note Upbeats

The hi-hat/cymbal part in this section is now played on the "&" of every beat. Play on the bell of the cymbal for the best effect. Omit the left foot hi-hat part if you have difficulty with these patterns. Go back and add the hi-hat part once you've mastered the three-way independence.

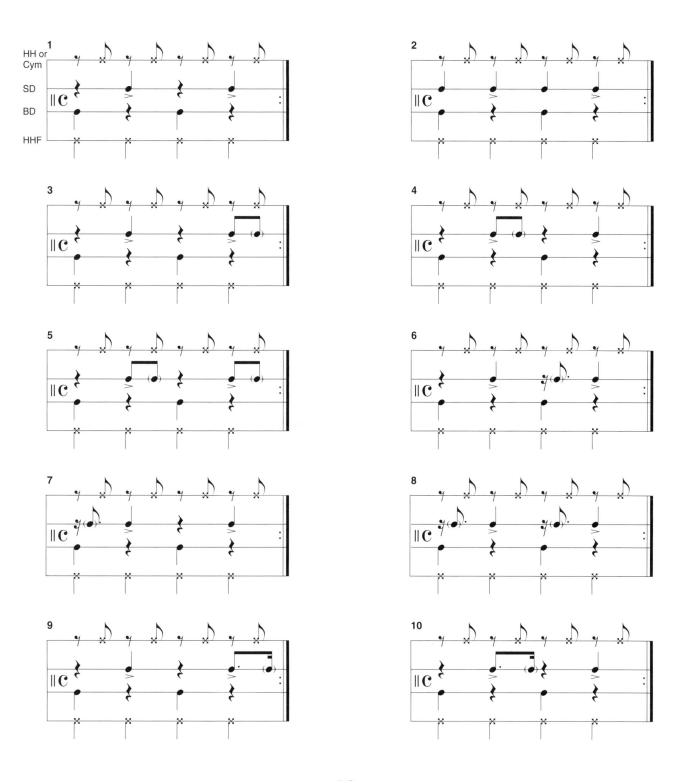

Progressive Independence: Rock

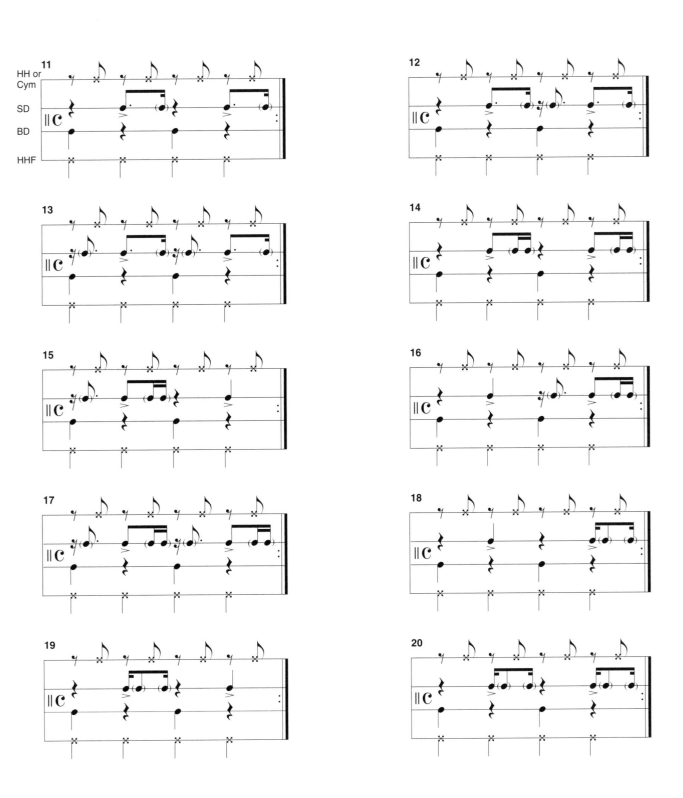

SECTION 3

Progressive Independence: Rock

Part 2: Bass Drum Independence With 8th-Note Upbeats

In Part 2 we'll work on the same bass drum variations used previously, now with the cymbal part on the "&" of every beat. Be sure to play each exercise slowly at first, practice with a metronome or drum machine, and keep a solid bass drum throughout.

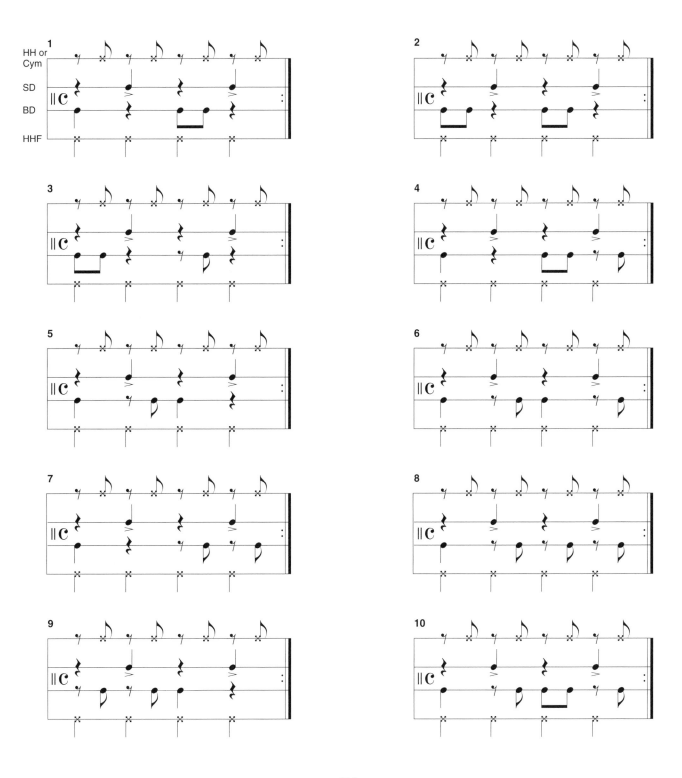

Progressive Independence: Rock

63

SECTION 3

Part 3: Snare Drum/Bass Drum Combinations

The focus here is on 8th-note upbeats combined with the snare drum and bass drum combinations from the previous two parts. Do not move on to the next exercise until you've mastered the previous one.

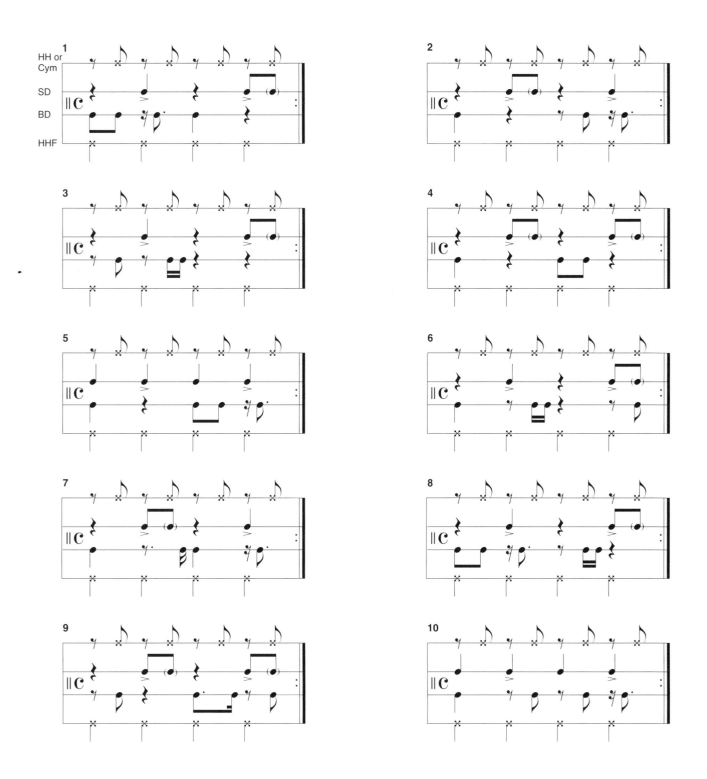

Progressive Independence: Rock

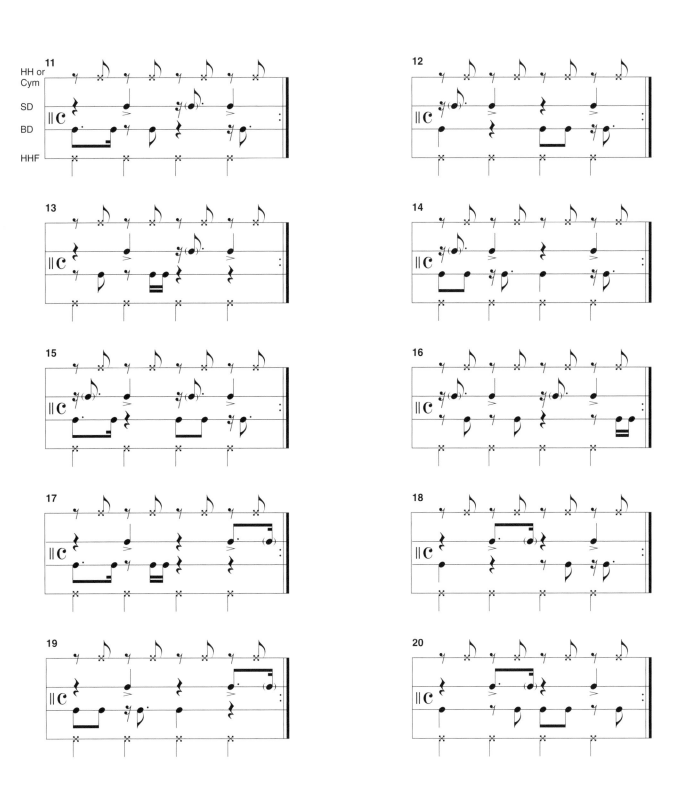

65

SECTION 3

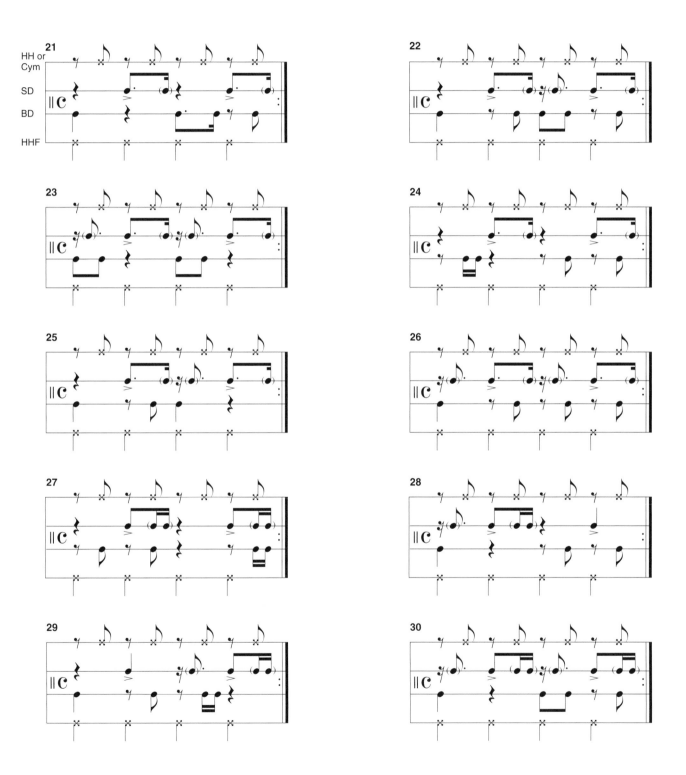

Progressive Independence: Rock

SECTION 3

Progressive Independence: Rock

SECTION 3

Part 4: Snare Drum/Bass Drum Combination Patterns With Hi-Hat 8th Notes

The following patterns combine the previous snare drum/bass drum combination patterns, now with the hi-hat playing 8th notes throughout. Take your time with this material, particularly during the latter part, when the exercises become increasingly complex.

Progressive Independence: Rock

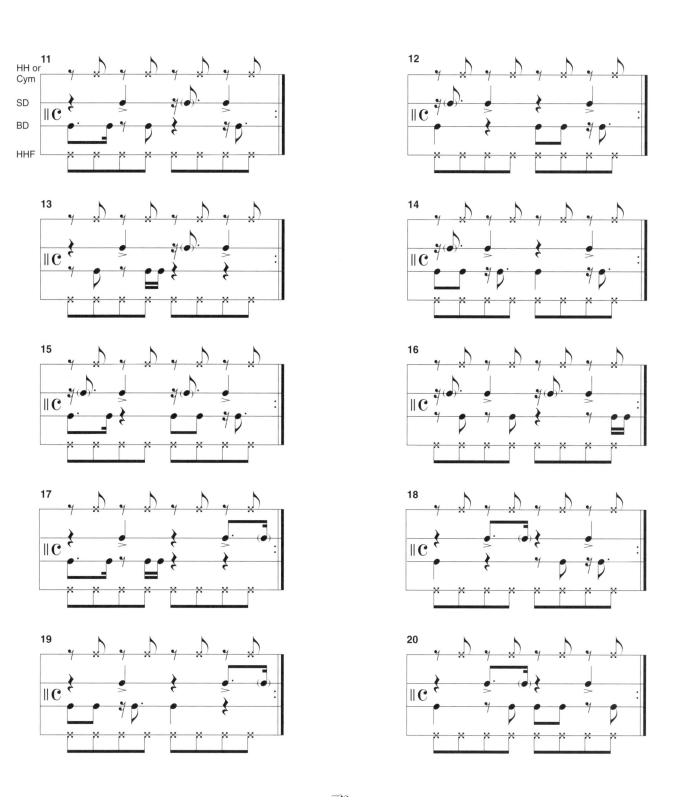

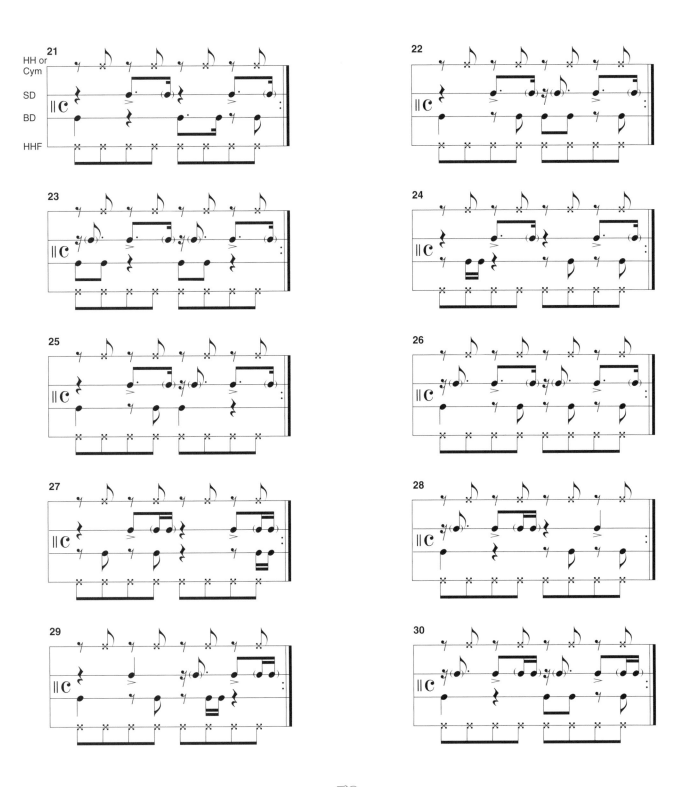

Progressive Independence: Rock

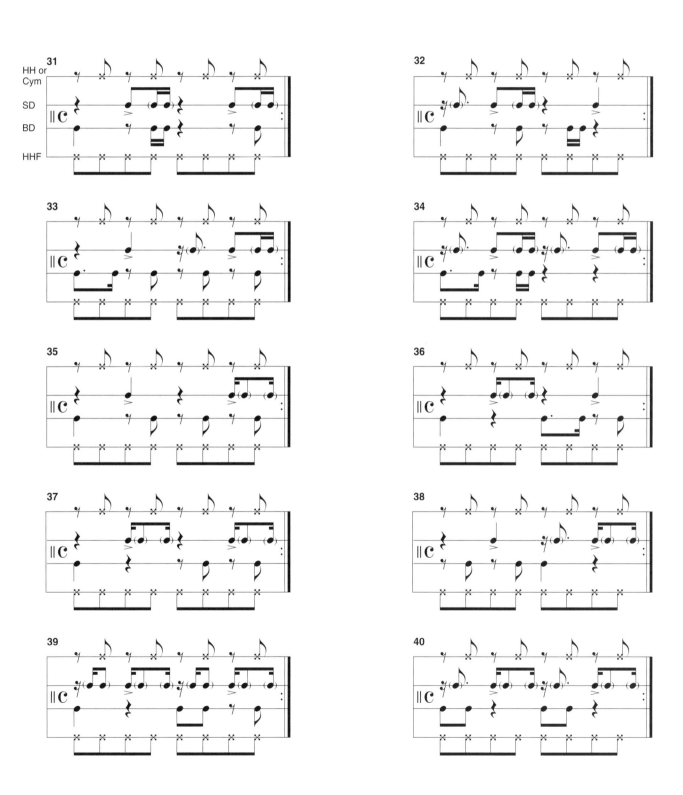

SECTION 3

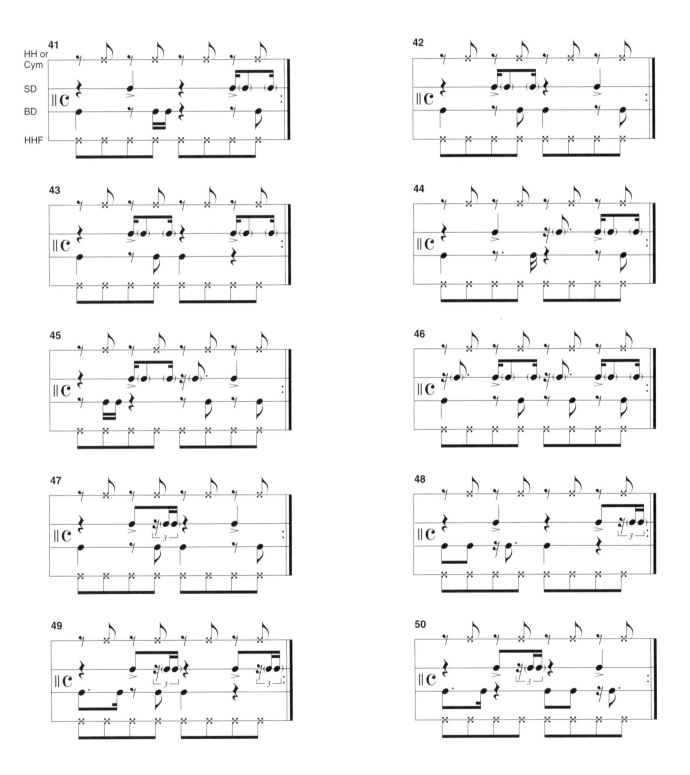

Progressive Independence: Rock

SECTION 3

Part 5: Snare Drum/Bass Drum Combination Patterns With Hi-Hat Upbeats

Part 5 once again involves the use of upbeat 8th notes in the hi-hat foot part. These patterns can be challenging, so take your time. Use a metronome or drum machine to ensure a steady, even time flow. Repeat each pattern ten to fifteen times before moving on.

Progressive Independence: Rock

SECTION 3

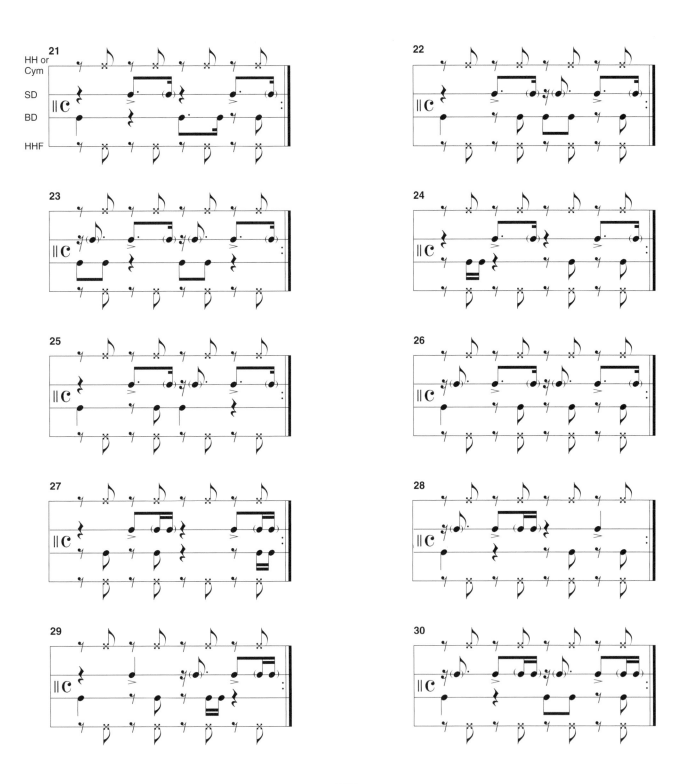

Progressive Independence: Rock

SECTION 3

Progressive Independence: Rock

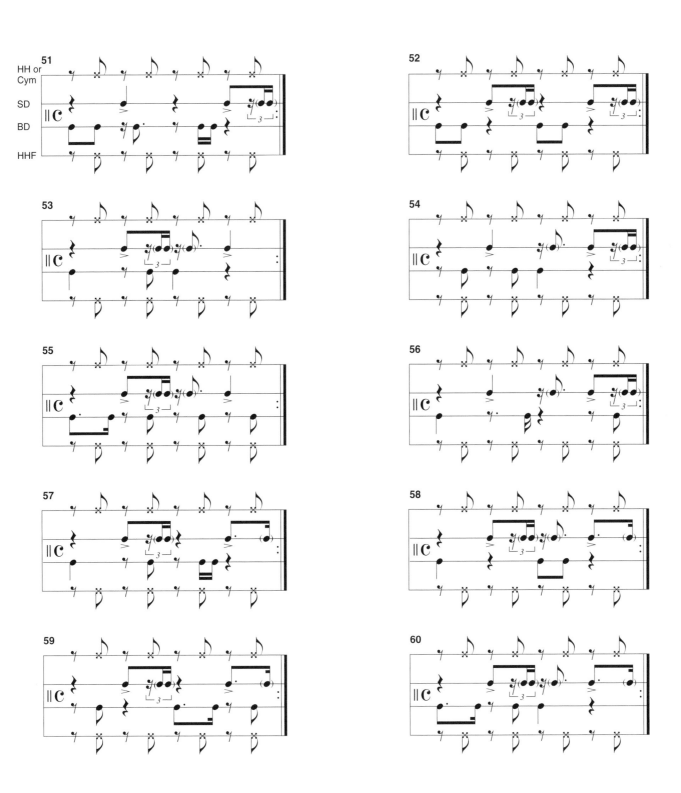

SECTION 3

Part 6: Two-Bar Combinations

The following patterns are two-bar combinations of the previous material. Exercises 1 through 5 begin with hi-hat quarter notes. Practice these slowly at first, gradually increasing the tempo as your facility increases.

The five two-bar combination patterns below utilize hi-hat 8th notes.

Exercises 11 through 15 on this page have the hi-hat foot playing upbeat 8th notes.

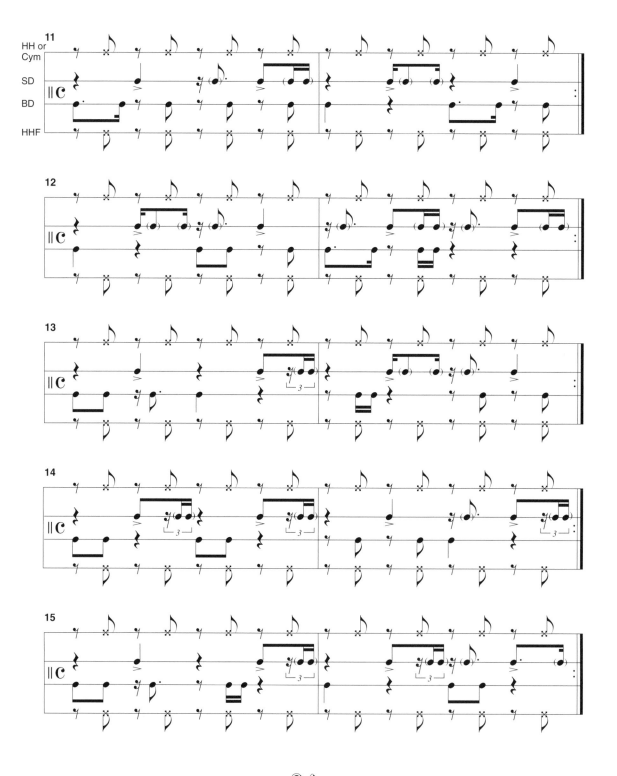

Progressive Independence: Rock

SECTION 4
Part 1: Snare Drum Independence With 16th Notes

Playing sixteen notes per bar places considerable stress on the hand, so practice all the exercises in this section *slower* than the previous material.

Note: All the patterns in Section 4 should be practiced two ways: 1) straight 16th notes as written, and 2) with more of a "swing-shuffle" feel, as shown below. Be sure to play all of the exercises in this section *both* ways.

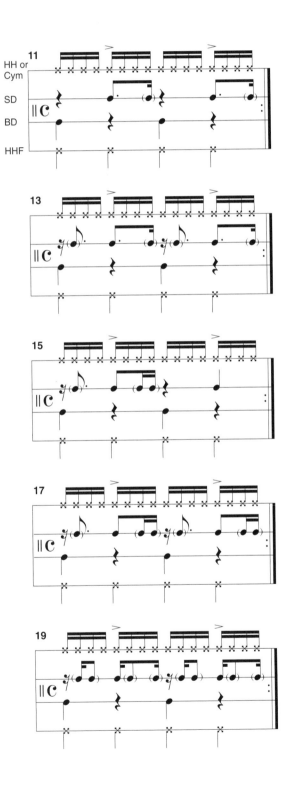
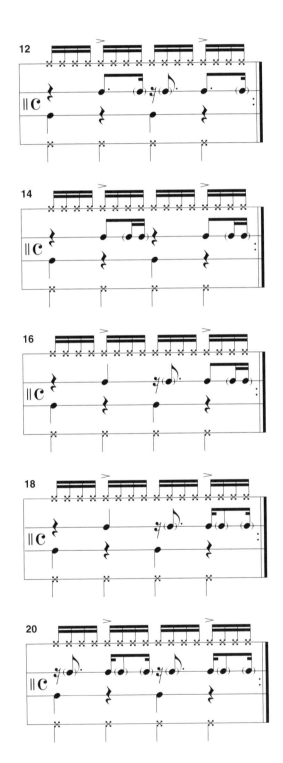

Progressive Independence: Rock

Part 2: Bass Drum Independence With 16th Notes

Now let's combine straight 16th notes with the thirty bass drum patterns. Be sure all bass drum notes fall in line accurately with the hand part.

Note: Another way to practice these exercises is to play the 16th notes on closed hi-hat using alternate single sticking, bringing the right hand to the snare drum on 2 and 4. See the examples below. Be sure to *omit* the hi-hat quarter notes when practicing the patterns in this manner.

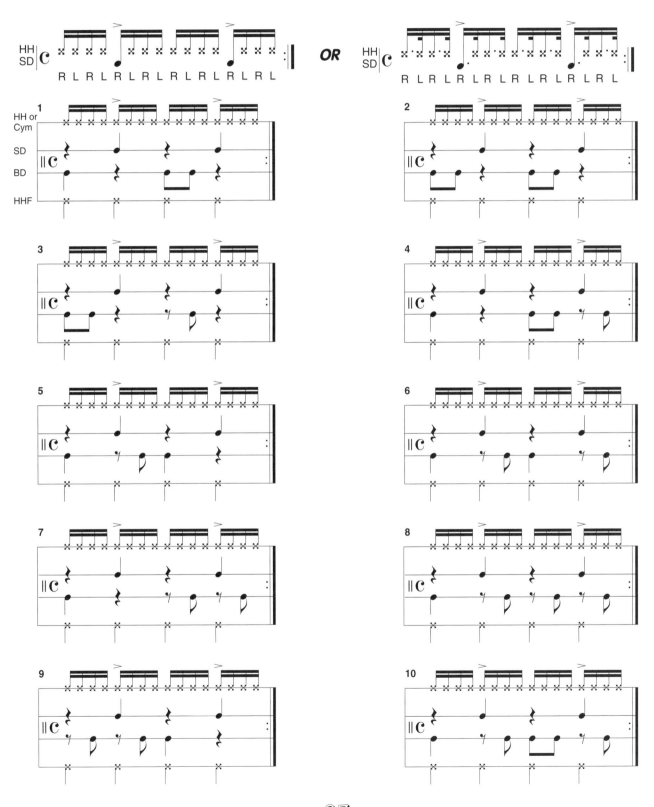

Progressive Independence: Rock

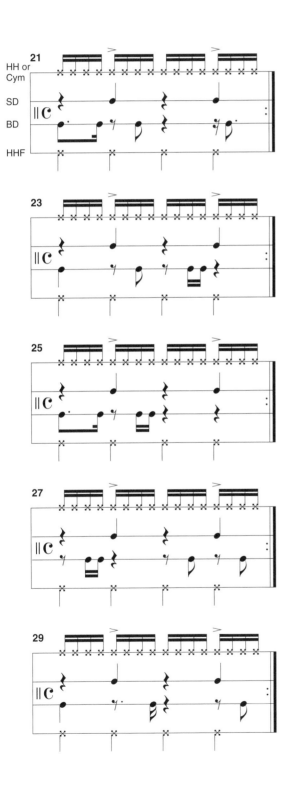
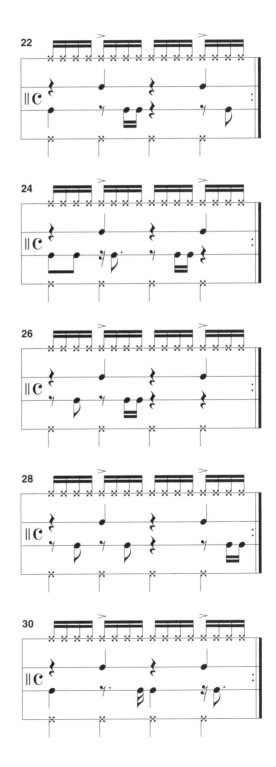

89

Part 3: Snare Drum/Bass Drum Combination Patterns

The sixty combination patterns that follow can be quite challenging. Practice them slowly, and remember that 2 and 4 are the emphasis points in every exercise. Ghost notes should always be played much softer. Strive for the proper balance among all the parts.

Progressive Independence: Rock

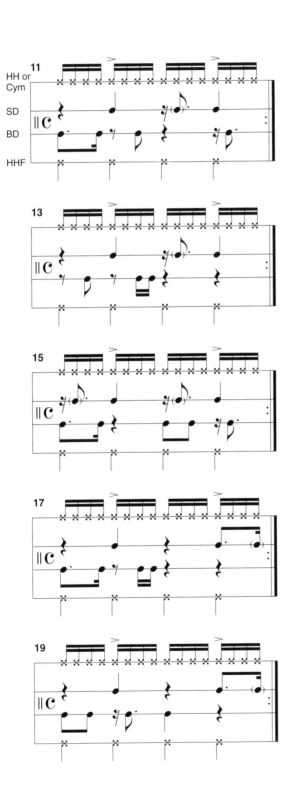
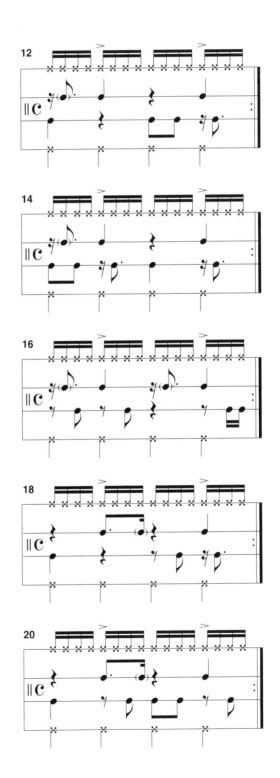

SECTION 4

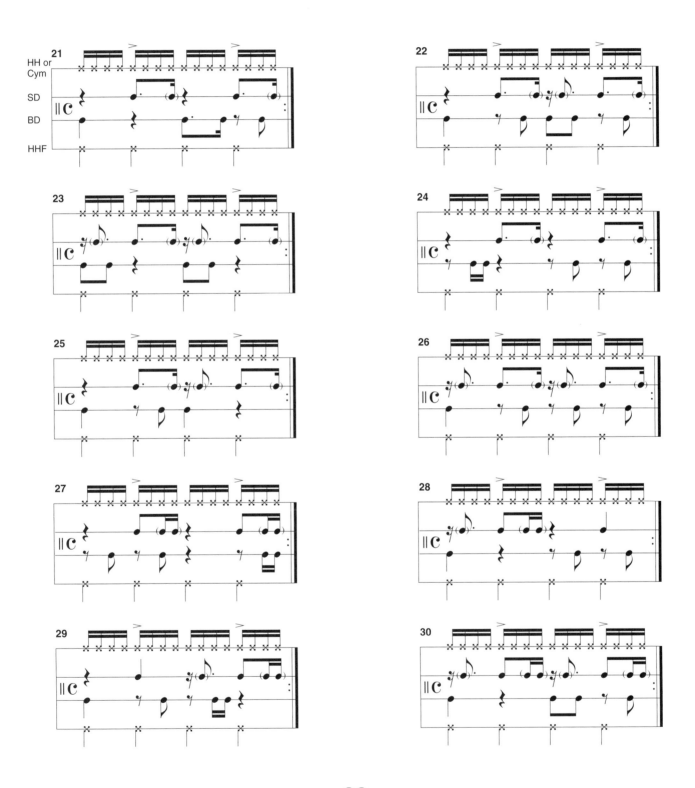

Progressive Independence: Rock

Progressive Independence: Rock

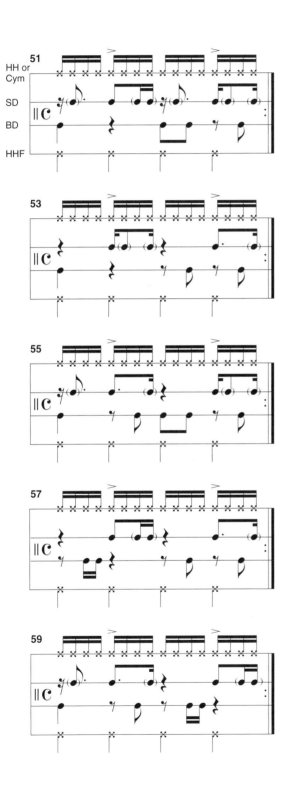
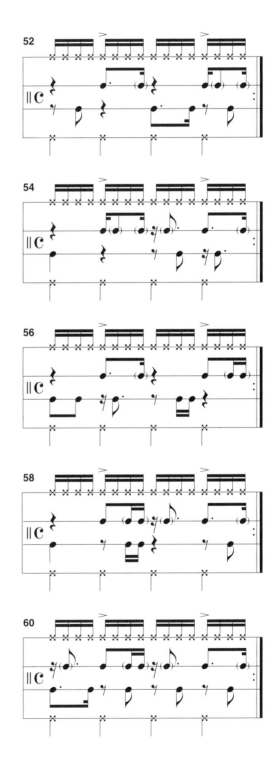

95

SECTION 4

Part 4: Snare Drum/Bass Drum Combination Patterns With Hi-Hat 8th Notes

Here are the same independence patterns from Part 3, now with 8th notes on the hi-hat. Be sure to rest at intervals should your cymbal hand begin to fatigue, or should the time begin to waver. The patterns in Part 4 require a good amount of endurance, control, and focus, so take your time.

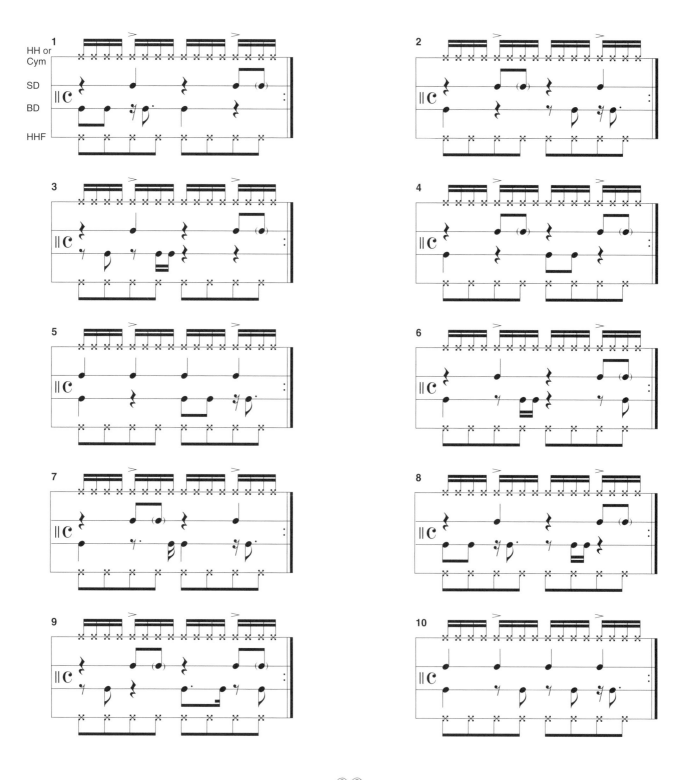

Progressive Independence: Rock

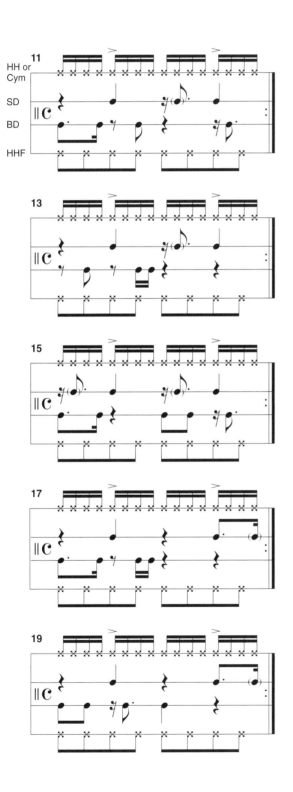
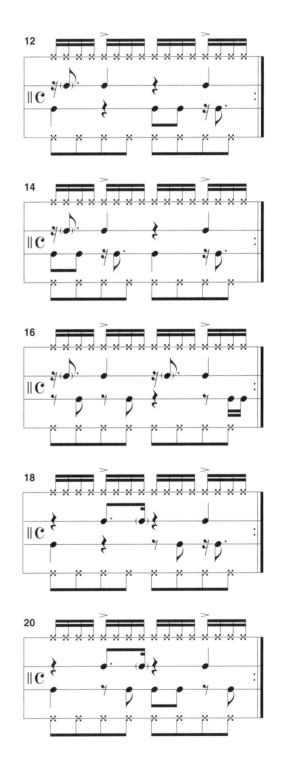

SECTION 4

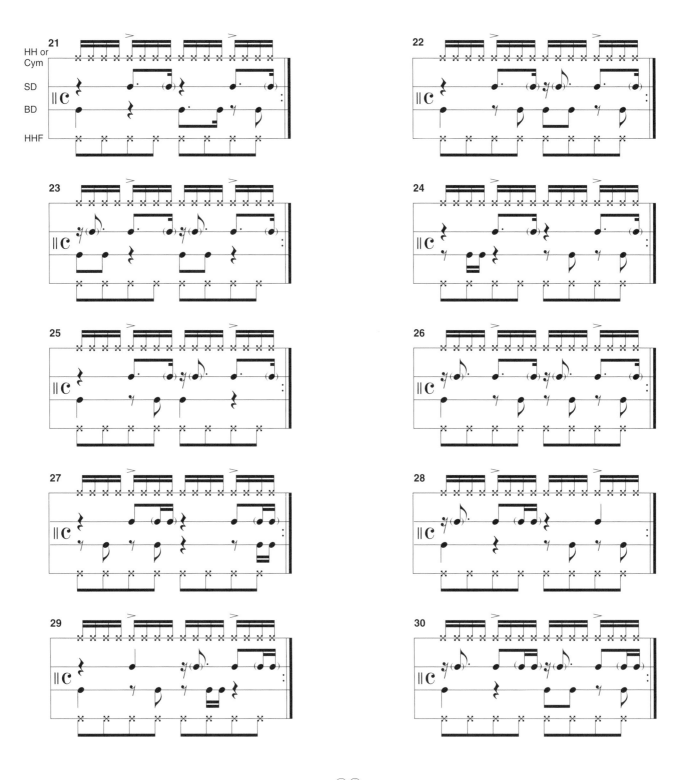

Progressive Independence: Rock

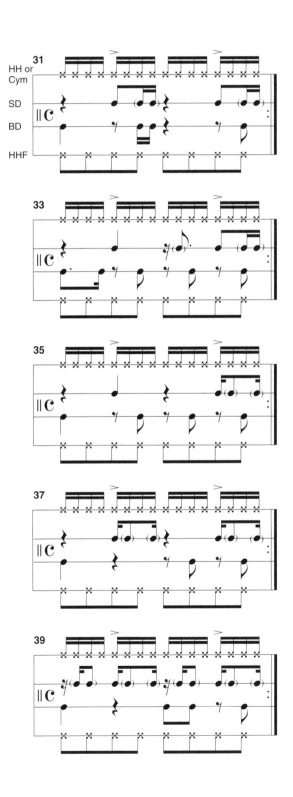
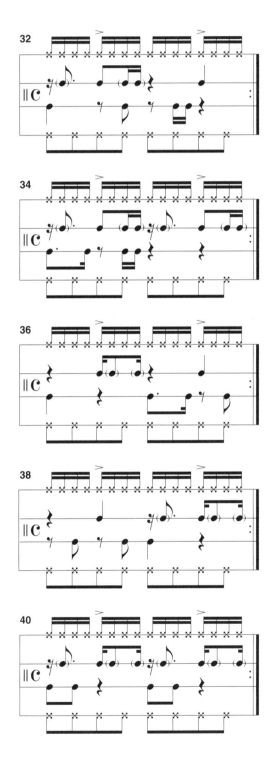

SECTION 4

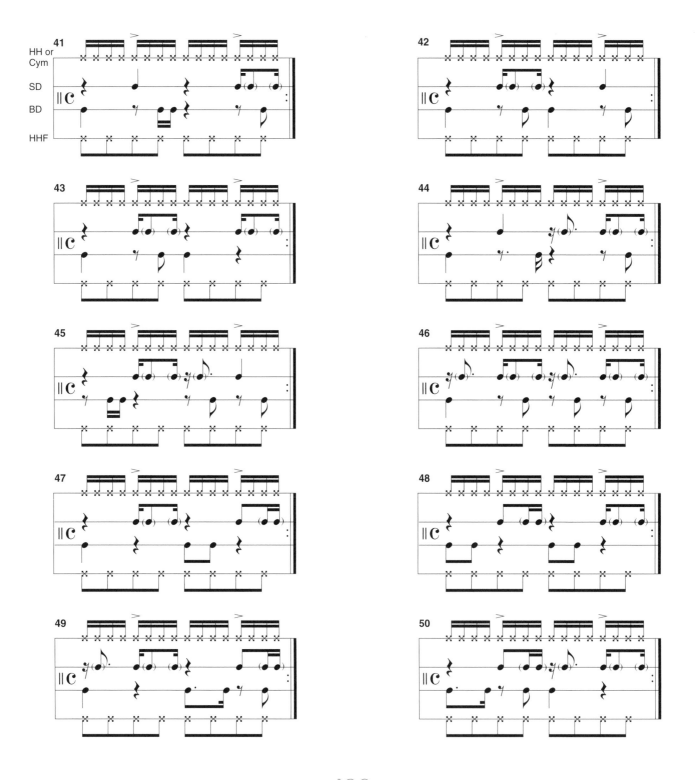

Progressive Independence: Rock

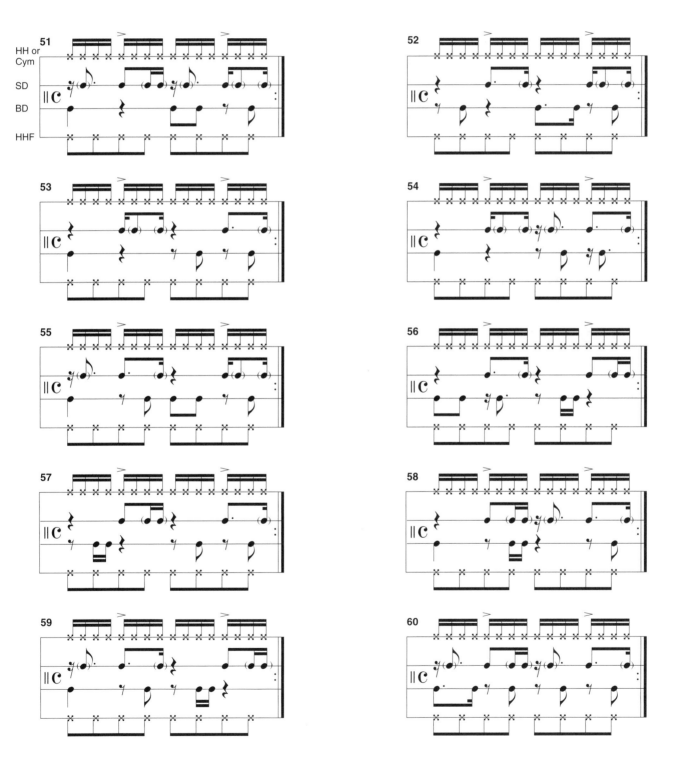

Part 5: Snare Drum/Bass Drum Combination Patterns With Hi-Hat Upbeats

In the final part of this section, 8th-note upbeats are utilized in the hi-hat foot. Practice each pattern slowly at first, and do not increase the tempo until you can play each exercise smoothly and accurately.

Progressive Independence: Rock

103

Progressive Independence: Rock

105

Progressive Independence: Rock

Part 6: Two-Bar Combinations

The following patterns are two-bar combinations of the previous material. Exercises 1 through 5 begin with hi-hat quarter notes. Practice these slowly at first, gradually increasing the tempo as your facility increases.

Progressive Independence: Rock

These five two-bar combination patterns utilize hi-hat 8th notes.

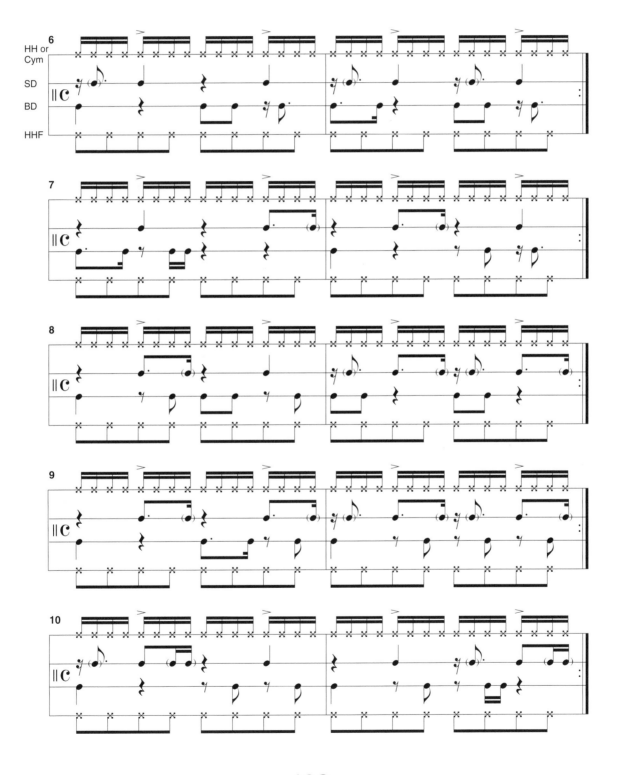

Exercises 11 through 15 have the hi-hat foot playing upbeat 8th notes.

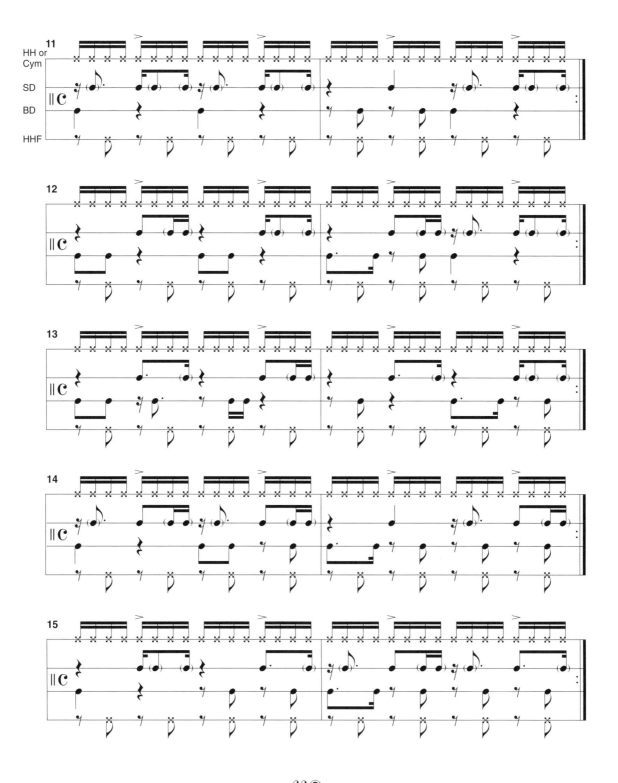

Progressive Independence: Rock

SECTION 5
Part 1: Snare Drum Independence With 16th-Note Figure A

The 16th-note figure used in the following thirty exercises is quite common. Feel free to omit the left foot hi-hat part the first time through this section if you experience difficulty. Go back and add it after you've mastered the three-way independence.

Note: Again, all the patterns in this Section should be practiced two ways: 1) the straight 16th-note figure as written, and 2) with more of a "swing-shuffle" feel, as shown below. Be sure to play all of the exercises in this section *both* ways.

Progressive Independence: Rock

Part 2: Bass Drum Independence With 16th-Note Figure A

Here are the same thirty bass drum patterns with 16th-note Figure A. Remember, accuracy is always more important than speed. Strive for precise execution and a good balance among all four limbs.

Progressive Independence: Rock

SECTION 5

Progressive Independence: Rock

Part 3: Snare Drum/Bass Drum Combination Patterns With 16th-Note Figure A

These combination patterns are complex and should be worked on carefully and methodically. By this point, the cymbal and hi-hat parts should feel relatively natural, allowing you to devote full concentration to the snare drum and bass parts.

Progressive Independence: Rock

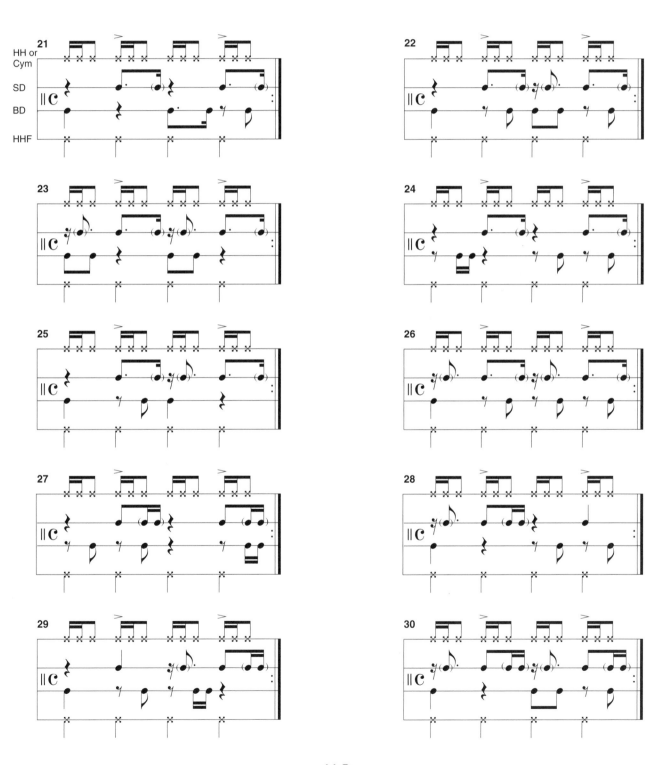

119

Progressive Independence: Rock

SECTION 5

Progressive Independence: Rock

Part 4: Snare Drum/Bass Drum Combination Patterns With Hi-Hat 8th Notes

Part 4 adds hi-hat 8th notes to the same patterns in Part 3. If you're still having difficulty with the independence, practice two or three of the four parts separately first (cymbal/bass drum; bass drum/hi-hat; cymbal/snare drum/bass drum) before attempting to play the complete pattern.

Progressive Independence: Rock

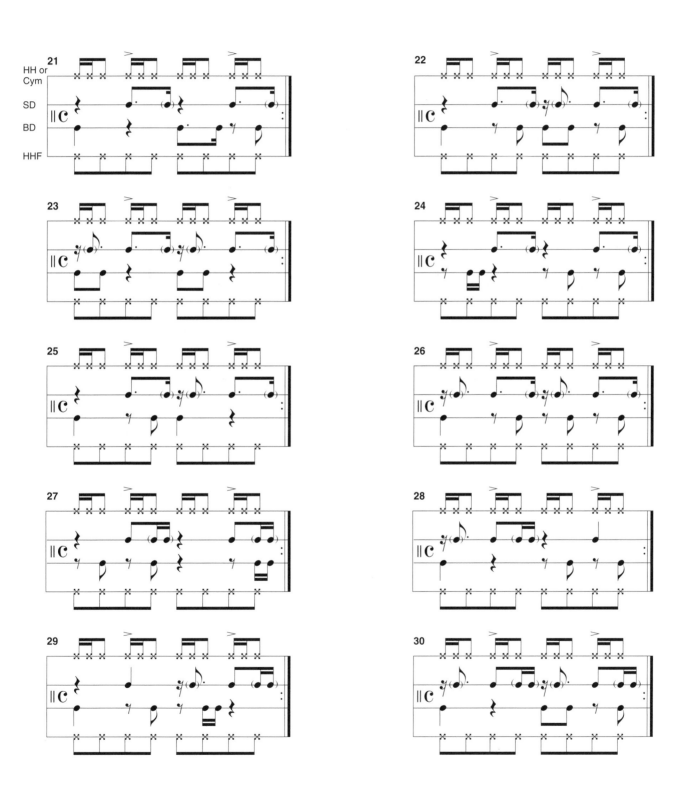

SECTION 5

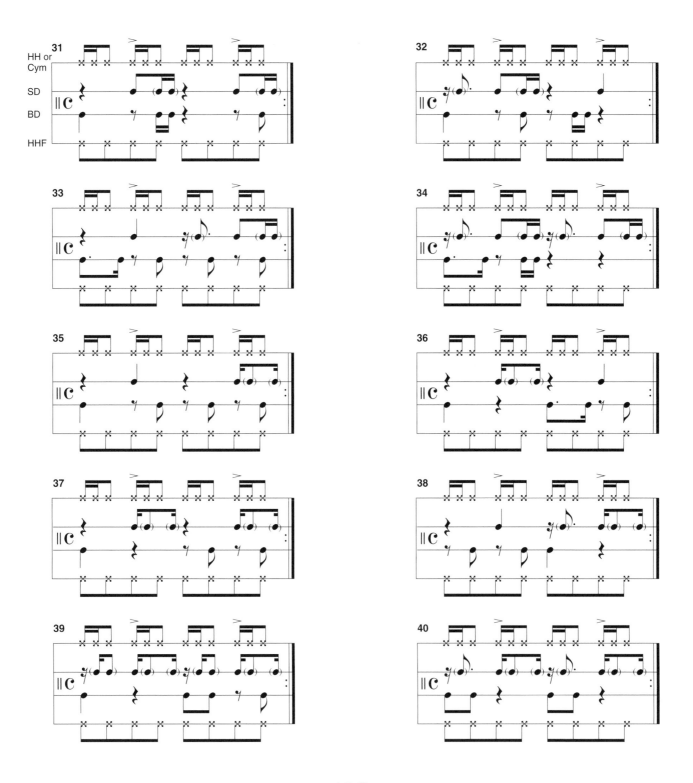

Progressive Independence: Rock

SECTION 5

Progressive Independence: Rock

Part 5: Snare Drum/Bass Drum Combination Patterns With Hi-Hat Upbeats

Part 5 once again involves the use of upbeat 8th notes in the hi-hat foot part. Repeat each pattern ten to fifteen times before moving on. All parts should fall naturally between the limbs, and each exercise should be played in a relaxed, musical manner.

Progressive Independence: Rock

131

SECTION 5

132

Progressive Independence: Rock

133

Progressive Independence: Rock

Part 6: Two-Bar Combinations

The following patterns are two-bar combinations of the previous material. Exercises 1 through 5 below begin with hi-hat quarter notes. Practice these exercises slowly at first, gradually increasing the tempo as your facility increases.

SECTION 5

The five two-bar combination patterns below utilize hi-hat 8th notes.

Progressive Independence: Rock

Exercises 11 through 15 have the hi-hat foot playing upbeat 8th notes.

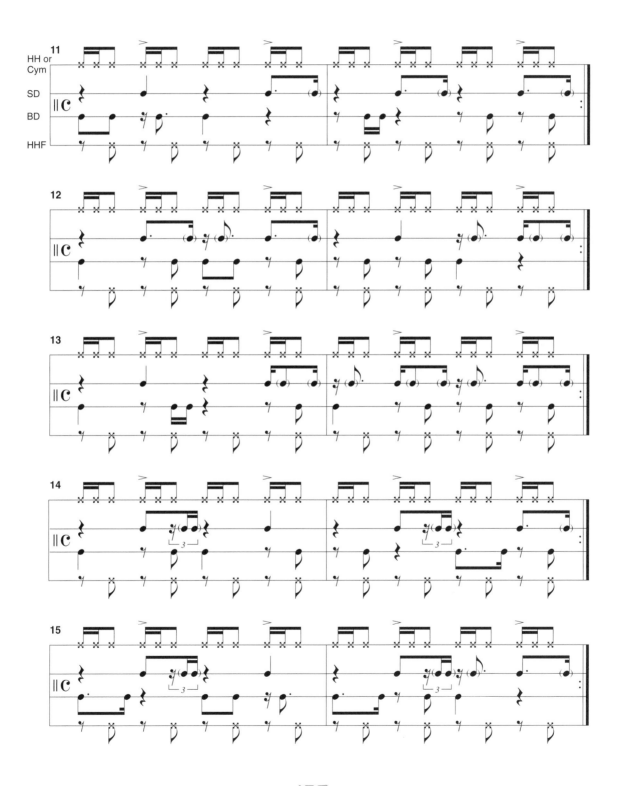

SECTION 6
Part 1: Snare Drum Independence With 16th-Note Figure B

In this final section, another common 16th-note figure is used. Practice it separately with just bass drum and hi-hat before adding the snare drum part.

Note: Once again, all the patterns in this section should be practiced first with a straight 16th-note feel and then with the "swing-shuffle" feel shown below. Practice all exercises both ways.

Progressive Independence: Rock

Part 2: Bass Drum Independence With 16th-Note Figure B

Be especially careful of the alignment between the hi-hat/cymbal and bass drum parts here. Be sure you've fully mastered each exercise before proceeding to the next one.

Progressive Independence: Rock

Progressive Independence: Rock

Part 3: Snare Drum/Bass Drum Combination Patterns With 16th-Note Figure B

The interplay between hi-hat/cymbal and snare drum in Part 3 can be tricky. Work each pattern out slowly, and maintain a strong bass drum with steady hi-hat quarter notes. Don't increase the tempo until you're totally comfortable with the four-way independence.

Progressive Independence: Rock

145

SECTION 6

Progressive Independence: Rock

Progressive Independence: Rock

Part 4: Snare Drum/Bass Drum Combination Patterns With Hi-Hat 8th Notes

The same sixty snare and bass drum combinations are used here, with the hi-hat now playing 8th notes throughout. Be sure to make a noticeable distinction between the accents on 2 and 4 and the ghost notes. Also, focus on maintaining a steady, even time flow through the use of a metronome or drum machine, and work on getting a good balance among all four parts.

149

SECTION 6

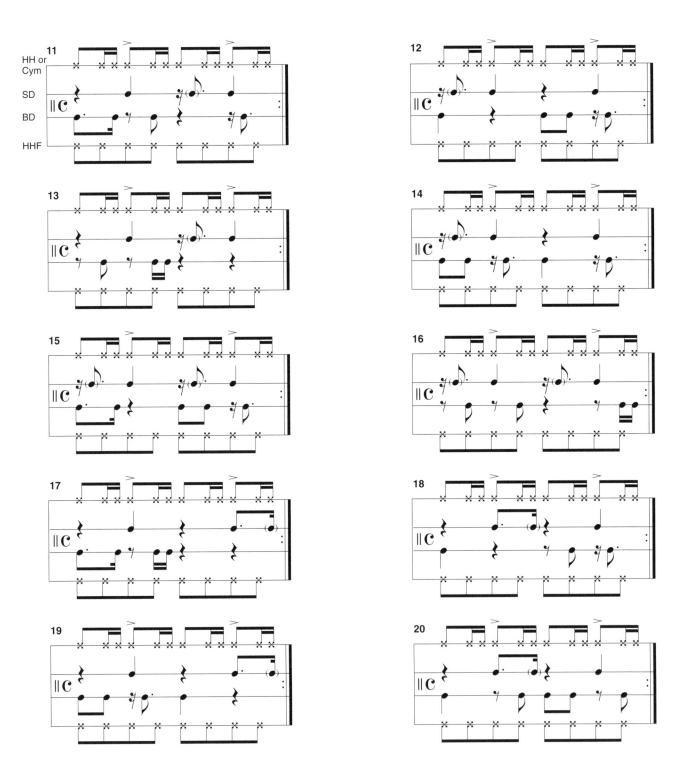

Progressive Independence: Rock

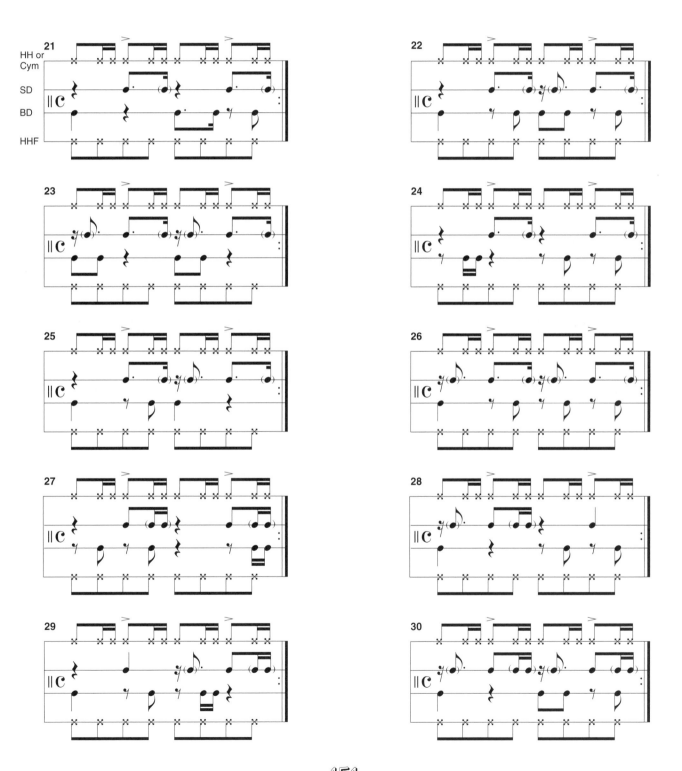

151

Progressive Independence: Rock

153

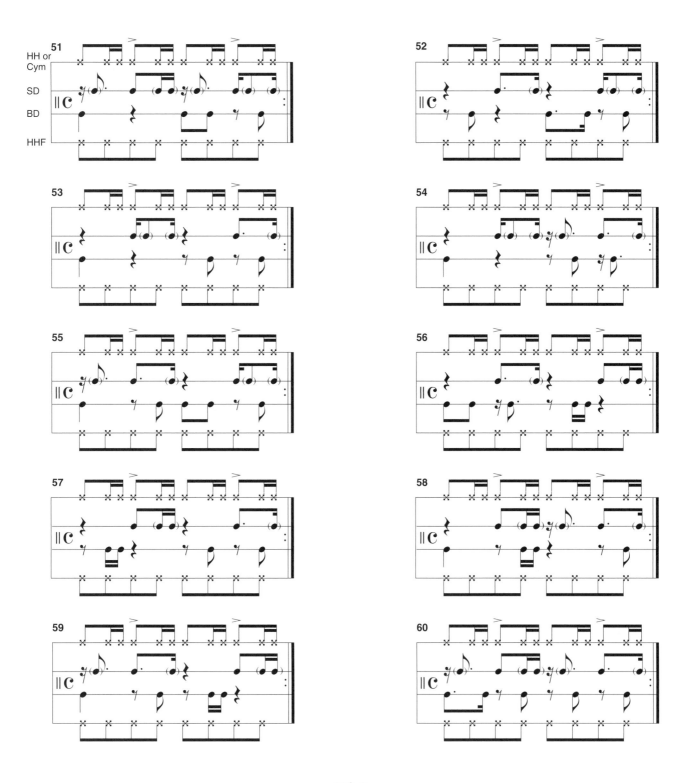

Progressive Independence: Rock

Part 5: Snare Drum/Bass Drum Combination Patterns With Hi-Hat Upbeats

This part once again involves the use of upbeat 8th notes in the hi-hat foot part. Repeat each pattern ten to fifteen times before moving on. Practice each pattern slowly at first and do not increase the tempo until each exercise can be played smoothly and accurately.

Progressive Independence: Rock

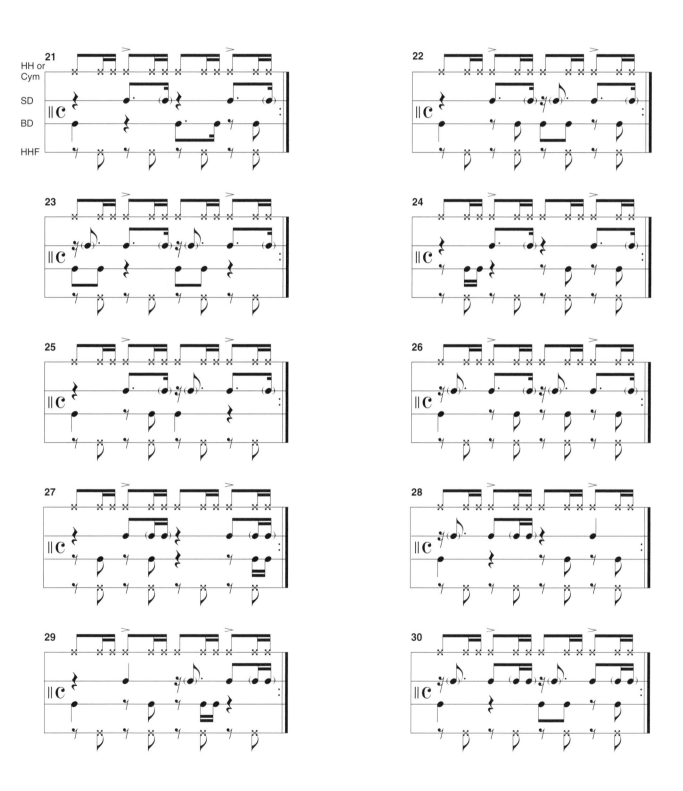

157

SECTION 6

Progressive Independence: Rock

159

SECTION 6

Progressive Independence: Rock

Part 6: Two-Bar Combinations

The following patterns are two-bar combinations of the previous material. Exercises 1 through 5 begin with hi-hat quarter notes. Practice these slowly at first, gradually increasing the tempo as your facility increases.

These five two-bar combination patterns utilize hi-hat 8th notes.

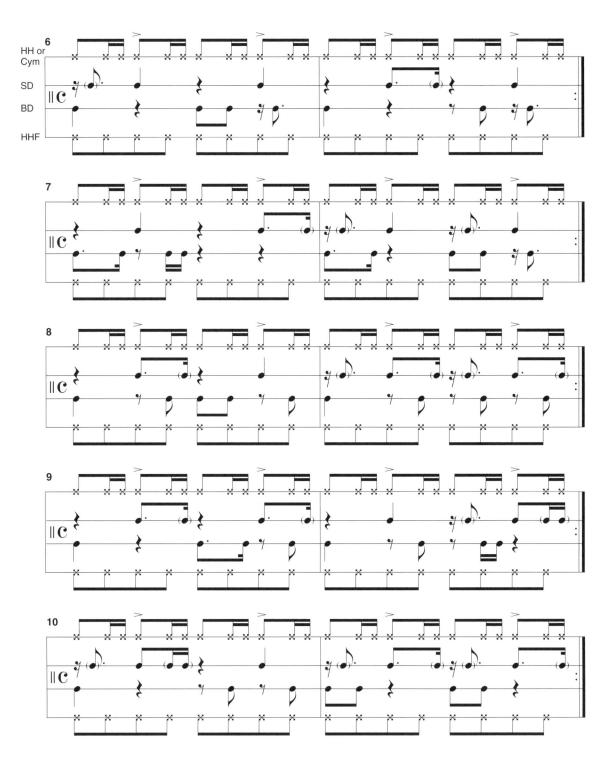

Progressive Independence: Rock

Exercises 11 through 15 have the hi-hat foot playing upbeat 8th notes.

CD Track Listing

* All examples recorded in Ableton Live, using FXpansion BFD2 drum production software and Modern Drummer Snare Drum Selects and Jazz & Funk sample libraries.

MAGAZINES · MULTI-MEDIA · ONLINE · EVENTS

www.moderndrummer.com